The Armed Forces

ISSUES

Volume 213

Series Editor

Lisa Firth

 *Independence*

Educational Publishers

Cambridge

First published by Independence

The Studio, High Green

Great Shelford

Cambridge CB22 5EG

England

© Independence 2011

British Library Cataloguing in Publication Data

The armed forces. -- (Issues ; v. 213)

1. Armed Forces. 2. Military policy.

I. Series II. Firth, Lisa.

355-dc23

ISBN-13: 978 1 86168 593 3

Printed in Great Britain

MWL Print Group Ltd

CONTENTS

Chapter 1 Military Matters

Frequently asked questions about the British Army	1
Service-related mental ill health	3
Servicemen in Iraq less stressed than emergency services in Britain	5
The UK Armed Forces – past, present and future	6
UK charities struggle to cope with wounded soldiers	7
'Surgery saved my hand after bomb blast'	8
Deaths in the UK regular Armed Forces	9
'I lost my leg in Iraq'	10
MoD completes review into women in close combat	12
Bearing babies and bearing arms is always incompatible	13
Catch 16–22	15
Under 18s' right of discharge	16
Strategic Defence and Security Review published	17
The Strategic Defence and Security Review: a criticism	20
It's time for Britain to merge its Army, Navy and Air Force	22
Armed Forces Covenant 'an historic breakthrough'	24
The Armed Forces Covenant	25
Some observations on the Armed Forces Covenant	26
Yes, we owe our Armed Forces – but Cameron's leaky law is not enough	28
What is the Territorial Army (TA)?	30

Chapter 2 Life After Service

Leaving the Armed Forces	31
Ex-military to be inspiring role models for young people	32
Veterans' mental health	33
MoD offers PTSD therapy	34
Veterans and homelessness	35
Ex-servicemen in prison	36
From hero to zero	37
Key Facts	40
Glossary	41
Index	42
Acknowledgements	43
Assignments	44

OTHER TITLES IN THE ISSUES SERIES

For more on these titles, visit: www.independence.co.uk

Sustainability and Environment ISBN 978 1 86168 419 6
A Classless Society? ISBN 978 1 86168 422 6
Migration and Population ISBN 978 1 86168 423 3
Sexual Orientation and Society ISBN 978 1 86168 440 0
The Gender Gap ISBN 978 1 86168 441 7
Domestic Abuse ISBN 978 1 86168 442 4
Travel and Tourism ISBN 978 1 86168 443 1
The Problem of Globalisation ISBN 978 1 86168 444 8
The Internet Revolution ISBN 978 1 86168 451 6
An Ageing Population ISBN 978 1 86168 452 3
Poverty and Exclusion ISBN 978 1 86168 453 0
Waste Issues ISBN 978 1 86168 454 7
Staying Fit ISBN 978 1 86168 455 4
Drugs in the UK ISBN 978 1 86168 456 1
The AIDS Crisis ISBN 978 1 86168 468 4
Bullying Issues ISBN 978 1 86168 469 1
Marriage and Cohabitation ISBN 978 1 86168 470 7
Our Human Rights ISBN 978 1 86168 471 4
Privacy and Surveillance ISBN 978 1 86168 472 1
The Animal Rights Debate ISBN 978 1 86168 473 8
Body Image and Self-Esteem ISBN 978 1 86168 484 4
Abortion – Rights and Ethics ISBN 978 1 86168 485 1
Racial and Ethnic Discrimination ISBN 978 1 86168 486 8
Sexual Health ISBN 978 1 86168 487 5
Selling Sex ISBN 978 1 86168 488 2
Citizenship and Participation ISBN 978 1 86168 489 9
Health Issues for Young People ISBN 978 1 86168 500 1
Crime in the UK ISBN 978 1 86168 501 8
Reproductive Ethics ISBN 978 1 86168 502 5
Tackling Child Abuse ISBN 978 1 86168 503 2
Money and Finances ISBN 978 1 86168 504 9
The Housing Issue ISBN 978 1 86168 505 6
Teenage Conceptions ISBN 978 1 86168 523 0
Work and Employment ISBN 978 1 86168 524 7
Understanding Eating Disorders ISBN 978 1 86168 525 4
Student Matters ISBN 978 1 86168 526 1
Cannabis Use ISBN 978 1 86168 527 8
Health and the State ISBN 978 1 86168 528 5
Tobacco and Health ISBN 978 1 86168 539 1
The Homeless Population ISBN 978 1 86168 540 7
Coping with Depression ISBN 978 1 86168 541 4
The Changing Family ISBN 978 1 86168 542 1
Bereavement and Grief ISBN 978 1 86168 543 8
Endangered Species ISBN 978 1 86168 544 5
Responsible Drinking ISBN 978 1 86168 555 1
Alternative Medicine ISBN 978 1 86168 560 5

Censorship Issues ISBN 978 1 86168 558 2
Living with Disability ISBN 978 1 86168 557 5
Sport and Society ISBN 978 1 86168 559 9
Self-Harming and Suicide ISBN 978 1 86168 556 8
Sustainable Transport ISBN 978 1 86168 572 8
Mental Wellbeing ISBN 978 1 86168 573 5
Child Exploitation ISBN 978 1 86168 574 2
The Gambling Problem ISBN 978 1 86168 575 9
The Energy Crisis ISBN 978 1 86168 576 6
Nutrition and Diet ISBN 978 1 86168 577 3
Coping with Stress ISBN 978 1 86168 582 7
Consumerism and Ethics ISBN 978 1 86168 583 4
Genetic Modification ISBN 978 1 86168 584 1
Education and Society ISBN 978 1 86168 585 8
The Media ISBN 978 1 86168 586 5
Biotechnology and Cloning ISBN 978 1 86168 587 2
International Terrorism ISBN 978 1 86168 592 6
The Armed Forces ISBN 978 1 86168 593 3
Vegetarian Diets ISBN 978 1 86168 594 0
Religion in Society ISBN 978 1 86168 595 7
Tackling Climate Change ISBN 978 1 86168 596 4
Euthanasia and Assisted Suicide ISBN 978 1 86168 597 1

A note on critical evaluation

Because the information reprinted here is from a number of different sources, readers should bear in mind the origin of the text and whether the source is likely to have a particular bias when presenting information (just as they would if undertaking their own research). It is hoped that, as you read about the many aspects of the issues explored in this book, you will critically evaluate the information presented. It is important that you decide whether you are being presented with facts or opinions. Does the writer give a biased or an unbiased report? If an opinion is being expressed, do you agree with the writer?

The Armed Forces offers a useful starting point for those who need convenient access to information about the many issues involved. However, it is only a starting point. Following each article is a URL to the relevant organisation's website, which you may wish to visit for further information.

Frequently asked questions about the British Army

Information from the Ministry of Defence.

Do soldiers get paid?

Yes. All soldiers get a wage that is closely linked to what they might be paid in civilian life. Extra allowances for things like going on operations or for doing certain types of job can help increase soldiers' wage packets even further.

Where do soldiers live?

The Army makes accommodation available for all its soldiers. Many people live in one-person rooms with en-suite bathrooms. This is called Z-class accommodation and new blocks of it are being completed all the time. The soldiers all pay rent, but this is at a much reduced rate compared to civilian housing.

Where do soldiers eat?

When they're based in barracks, soldiers have plenty of options. They can eat in one of the restaurants on the base or they can cook in one of the communal kitchens in their accommodation block. If soldiers live off the base in their own houses, they can eat on the base or cook for themselves.

What types of food are available?

Soldiers can eat exactly the same range of food as you get in civilian life. The restaurants on Army bases do everything from healthy options to occasional treats like chips and burgers. When soldiers are away from proper catering facilities, they eat from nutritionally balanced ration packs. There are many different types of these available, including halal, kosher and vegetarian.

Do all soldiers have to go on operations?

The chances are that anyone who joins the Army will have to go on operations at some point in their career. Soldiers work and train hard and the logical next step is that they put their skills to the ultimate test. They might not need to use their soldiering or trade skills, but everyone will have a part to play.

Can you have Muslim soldiers?

The Army has soldiers from all faiths and communities. There are Muslim soldiers as well as Jewish soldiers, Hindu soldiers and others from Britain and Commonwealth countries. The only thing that matters is that soldiers are prepared to work for each other and towards a common goal.

Can someone leave the Army if they want to?

Yes, but there are some restrictions.

If you're under 18 when you join, you can leave by giving 14 days' notice at any time after you've been in the Army for 28 days – provided this is within six months from the day you join.

Strength of UK Regular Forces by religion, 2010 (all services)[1]

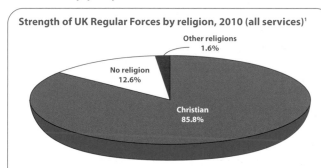

'Other religions' category (1.6%) consisting of:

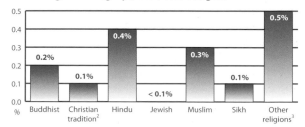

1. Percentages calculated from unrounded data and based on those with known religion only.
2. Christian tradition includes Christian Scientist, Church of Jesus Christ of Latter-Day Saints (Mormon), Jehovah's Witness and Unitarian religions among others.
3. Other religions includes Druid, Pagan, Rastafarian, Spiritualist Zoroastrian (Parsee), Wicca and Baha'i among others.

Source: Defence Analytical Services and Advice (DASA - Quad-Service), Crown copyright.

People who are over 18 when they join have to give 14 days' notice at any time after 28 days' service to leave within three months after joining. Soldiers who are still doing their basic training can leave with their commanding officer's permission.

What support is there for people who have left?

Soldiers who plan to leave the Army will complete a resettlement package which helps them readjust and develop the skills they need to find a job in civilian life. This includes everything from interview preparation to drawing up a CV. The qualifications that soldiers get in the Army are recognised by civilian employers and include things like NVQs and City & Guilds certificates, so they will have a head start in the job market. There are also many veterans' groups and charities who can provide expert help to former soldiers who are experiencing longer-term problems with their return to civilian life.

Soldiers who plan to leave the Army will complete a resettlement package which helps them readjust and develop the skills they need to find a job in civilian life

Are soldiers allowed to come home?

All soldiers get a minimum of 38 days' holiday each year. The Army calls this 'leave'. In practice the annual leave allowance will be increased if a soldier goes on operations or for a range of other reasons. When soldiers aren't on exercises or operations, they work a normal working day with regular hours. This leaves plenty of weekends and evenings free to see family and friends, no matter where they live. All the Army asks is that they're available to work when they're needed.

Can they keep in touch with friends and family?

People in the Army are actively encouraged to keep in touch. Most soldiers have mobile phones, which they're allowed to use provided it doesn't interfere with them doing their jobs. With many soldiers owning laptops, they'll also have access to email facilities in their own rooms, or using computers in the communal areas at their barracks. It's not quite so easy to stay in touch if a soldier is on operations, but there will be phones available on many bases and soldiers can send and receive mail.

What happens if a soldier gets injured?

It's the job of the Army Medical Services to keep soldiers fit, healthy and able to do their jobs. If a soldier receives a lasting injury which means they're unable to carry out their duties, then they may have to leave the Army. Depending on the circumstances of the injury and a range of other factors, there may be some financial compensation available.

Do soldiers get a pension?

Yes. After just two years' service, soldiers earn an Army pension that will be paid to them when they reach 65. If soldiers serve for 12 years they receive a tax-free resettlement grant when they retire. Anybody over 40 who has done at least 18 years in the Army gets an immediate pension, a tax-free lump sum and a second lump sum when they get to 65.

⇨ Information from the British Army. Visit www.army.mod.uk for more.

© Crown copyright

THE BRITISH ARMY

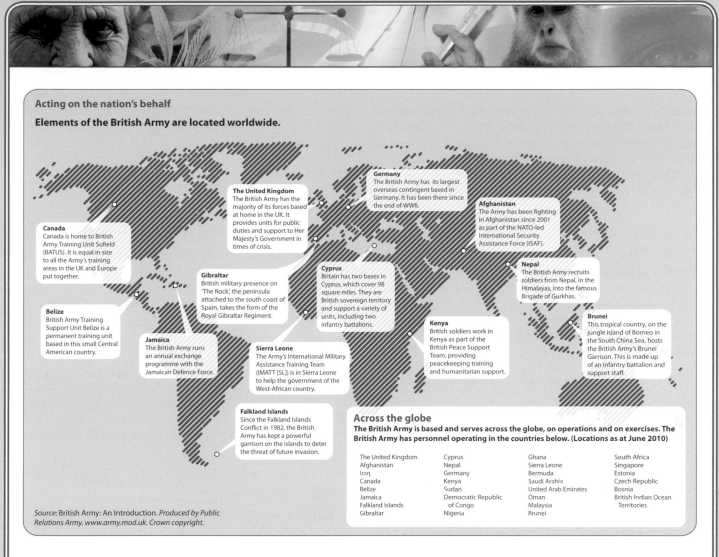

Acting on the nation's behalf

Elements of the British Army are located worldwide.

Canada
Canada is home to British Army Training Unit Sufield (BATUS). It is equal in size to all the Army's training areas in the UK and Europe put together.

Belize
British Army Training Support Unit Belize is a permanent training unit based in this small Central American country.

Jamaica
The British Army runs an annual exchange programme with the Jamaican Defence Force.

The United Kingdom
The British Army has the majority of its forces based at home in the UK. It provides units for public duties and support to Her Majesty's Government in times of crisis.

Gibraltar
British military presence on 'The Rock', the peninsula attached to the south coast of Spain, takes the form of the Royal Gibraltar Regiment.

Cyprus
Britain has two bases in Cyprus, which cover 98 square miles. They are British sovereign territory and support a variety of units, including two infantry battalions.

Sierra Leone
The Army's International Military Assistance Training Team (IMATT [SL]) is in Sierra Leone to help the government of the West-African country.

Falkland Islands
Since the Falkland Islands Conflict in 1982, the British Army has kept a powerful garrison on the islands to deter the threat of future invasion.

Germany
The British Army has its largest overseas contingent based in Germany. It has been there since the end of WWII.

Afghanistan
The Army has been fighting in Afghanistan since 2001 as part of the NATO-led International Security Assistance Force (ISAF).

Nepal
The British Army recruits soldiers from Nepal, in the Himalayas, into the famous Brigade of Gurkhas.

Kenya
British soldiers work in Kenya as part of the British Peace Support Team, providing peacekeeping training and humanitarian support.

Brunei
This tropical country, on the jungle island of Borneo in the South China Sea, hosts the British Army's Brunei Garrison. This is made up of an infantry battalion and support staff.

Across the globe
The British Army is based and serves across the globe, on operations and on exercises. The British Army has personnel operating in the countries below. (Locations as at June 2010)

The United Kingdom	Cyprus	Ghana	South Africa
Afghanistan	Nepal	Sierra Leone	Singapore
Iraq	Germany	Bermuda	Estonia
Canada	Kenya	Saudi Arabia	Czech Republic
Belize	Sudan	United Arab Emirates	Bosnia
Jamaica	Democratic Republic	Oman	British Indian Ocean
Falkland Islands	of Congo	Malaysia	Territories
Gibraltar	Nigeria	Brunei	

Source: British Army: An Introduction. *Produced by Public Relations Army. www.army.mod.uk. Crown copyright.*

Service-related mental ill health

Post-Traumatic Stress Disorder (PTSD): frequently asked questions.

Some people are sceptical about PTSD amongst our Armed Forces. Surely if you 'sign up' you should expect to see some terrible things?

Yes, of course service personnel expect to witness and be involved in extreme events, and to this extent PTSD could be viewed as an occupational hazard. They do, however, expect the condition to be recognised and dealt with appropriately. The problem is not helped if the sufferer does not recognise the problem he or she is experiencing or does not seek medical help.

How many of your clients have PTSD?

The commonest presentation in our patient group is PTSD, with our recent clinical audits showing that PTSD is the primary diagnosis in 75% of cases. Most of this PTSD is chronic in nature. In 62% of cases it is present co-morbidly with other disorders, especially depression, and a history of current or past alcohol abuse or dependence (addiction). Anxiety disorders, phobic disorders, problems with anger and problems which reflect personality change following exposure to catastrophe are also evident, as is illicit drug abuse and, more rarely, dependence (addiction).

Why is the NHS not treating people with PTSD?

It is, but the service appears to be patchy at present. With so many demands on the NHS, local facilities may not offer specialist trauma-focused services, or be able to manage veterans in a contextually sensitive environment. There are currently very few specialist services to meet the treatment needs of this veteran group.

In 2010, Combat Stress signed a partnership agreement with the MoD and the Department of Health: this aims to strengthen local NHS provision in areas where we know that a high proportion of veterans live. In England, Combat Stress is working with the DoH and the NHS to help set up regional veterans Mental Health Networks which it is hoped will provide clinical assessment delivered by Community Psychiatric Nurses, psychiatrists and psychologists from the NHS and that these services will dovetail with Combat Stress's Community Outreach service.

Combat Stress has also set up a national telephone helpline funded through the DoH. We have also helped to steer the Improving Access to Psychological Therapies services being set up nationally to highlight the special

needs of veterans with mental health disorders. We have also been awarded National Specialist Commissioning by the Department of Health in England to provide an intensive six-week treatment programme for veterans with complicated presentations of severe PTSD. This and similar programmes have been running successfully in Australia and treating veterans for the past 15 years.

Is there a particular type of person who is especially vulnerable to PTSD?

Some people are more resilient than others, but every individual has their breaking point and will have different responses to a traumatic incident. Exposure to multiple and sustained trauma, and lack of supportive structures (peer group and/or family support) increase the risk of developing PTSD.

How long does it take to show signs of PTSD?

In the immediate aftermath of a traumatic event, it is normal for people to experience some of the typical symptoms of PTSD. However, if symptoms are prolonged for more than one month, a clinical diagnosis of PTSD might be made. Many people may not report or even recognise the symptoms they are suffering from as trauma – or service-related. An individual may suffer for years in silence before finally trying to get treatment. Often the death of a spouse, loss of a job, or anniversaries such as Remembrance Day can be the final straw that leads the veteran to ask for help.

Delayed-onset PTSD is rarer. In these cases PTSD presents many months or years after traumatic exposure, with no history of any prior mental health symptoms. Recent studies show that delayed-onset PTSD is more common after the serviceman or woman has left the military, and usually manifests in the first year after discharge. Delayed-onset PTSD is also more common in the veteran population than it is among civilians.

What is the average length of time it takes for veterans with mental health problems to seek YOUR help?

Our latest figures show that it takes around 13 years from service discharge to making first contact with Combat Stress.

Is PTSD curable?

PTSD is easier to treat the earlier the person presents with it. The longer it has been present, the more chronic it becomes and the more difficult it is to treat. Many patients do well because they persevere in therapy and do not give up. It is important to be patient, and not expect an illness that has been present for many years to be cured within a few weeks or months.

Is PTSD the only response to trauma?

No. In fact PTSD is not the commonest disorder that can develop. People can develop a whole range of other problems, which can exist alone or co-exist with their PTSD. Anxiety symptoms, depression, use of alcohol and illicit drugs, problems with relationships, work and family function are common. In addition, exposure to severe stress may exacerbate physical illnesses, such as some skin complaints, as well as chronic pain.

How do veterans find their way to you?

Referrals come from a wide variety of sources – directly from veterans themselves, the War Pensions Welfare service, service charities and regimental associations, medical, health and social services, and family and friends.

How do you help the families and friends of PTSD sufferers?

Our Community Outreach teams frequently come into contact with the family and offer advice and support. We have a small number of beds available at Audley Court Hollybush House and Tyrwhitt House so that carers can come with the veterans.

We have also established a number of Carer Support Groups around the UK.

What are you doing to help veterans in prison, especially those who reportedly have PTSD?

Combat Stress accepts referrals from those with six months or less of their sentence to complete. We provide welfare support and treatment to veterans on their release. Combat Stress is also a leading member of 'Prison In-Reach'. This is a government initiative, working in partnership with ex-service organisations, to recognise the special difficulties veterans have both during their sentence and on release.

Does Combat Stress treat serving members of the Armed Forces?

Our clinical treatments are limited to veterans of the British Armed Forces. However, while we predominantly care for veterans and their families, we have launched the Combat Stress 24-Hour Helpline for the whole military community. The helpline provides support and can signpost serving personnel, veterans and their families to relevant organisations. Serving personnel with concerns about their mental health are advised to seek help from the service health authorities and other relevant organisations that might be able to help with their situation.

11 August 2011

⇨ The above information is reprinted with kind permission from Combat Stress. Visit their website at www.combatstress.org.uk for more information on this and other related issues.

COMBAT STRESS

Servicemen in Iraq less stressed than emergency services in Britain

Britain's Armed Forces serving in Iraq show less signs of psychological distress than police officers, doctors in emergency departments and disaster workers, a study has found.

By Richard Alleyne, Science Correspondent

Psychologists discovered that just over one in five servicemen on deployment showed signs of psychological distress and less than four per cent showed signs of post-traumatic stress disorder (PTSD).

These levels of mental health are the same as soldiers, sailors and airmen in training and less than those in other high-stress occupations, such as police officers, doctors in emergency departments and disaster workers.

Focusing on the mental health of UK Armed Forces while on deployment, the study by researchers at the Institute of Psychiatry, King's College London, included servicemen and women at eight locations across Iraq in January and February 2009.

Of the 611 surveyed, 20.5 per cent demonstrated symptoms of psychological distress, while 3.4 per cent showed signs of PTSD.

Respondents were more likely to report good health if they were of officer rank, if they felt their unit was very cohesive and had supportive leadership, and if they had taken a period of rest and recuperation in an area outside an operational theatre.

Those who reported psychological distress were most likely to be young, female, in the Army, and of junior rank.

Personnel belonging to junior ranks were also more likely to show symptoms of PTSD, along with those who felt they were in danger of being killed.

The report showed that sickness levels were very low, with only 1.6 per cent of personnel taking more than three days off during their six-month deployment.

While a lot of research on the mental health of UK Armed Forces personnel has been conducted either before or after deployment, very little is known about their mental health during deployment, Professor Neil Greenberg from the Academic Centre for Defence Mental Health said.

'Interestingly, those who told us they remembered having a pre-deployment stress briefing reported significantly better mental health than those who did not,' he said.

Although most units had medical support, Professor Greenberg said training for medical staff had only recently begun to be standardised to ensure it covered mental health disorders.

'Improving training, as well as raising awareness among staff of the link between these personnel reporting sick and having poorer mental health, may help identify those in most need of psychological help,' he said.

Those who took part in the survey, published in the *British Journal of Psychiatry*, represented about 15 per cent of personnel deployed in Iraq at the time.

29 October 2010

THE TELEGRAPH

The UK Armed Forces – past, present and future

Information from the Institute of Psychiatry, King's College London.

Occurrence of mental health problems amongst Army personnel can only be reduced or better managed, but never eliminated. These are the findings of a paper published today, which also stresses the need for further research to gauge why some service personnel suffer whilst others don't.

Scientists from the King's Centre for Military Health Research (KCMHR) examined the historical and contemporary evidence to explain the inconsistencies in rates of psychological injuries. They also provide an insight into some of the ways that the UK Armed Forces attempt to mitigate the effects of operations upon personnel's mental health.

Researchers found that the UK Armed Forces employ tactics to equip personnel with better coping methods, such as third location decompression (TLD), which means the troops spend 24–36 hours in a neutral space to 'unwind' together, and trauma risk management (TRiM), which provides personnel with the skills to monitor how other troops are coping.

A comparison study between UK and US Armed Forces proved that US personnel suffered higher rates of psychological ill health, presumably because US personnel are deployed for longer and more frequently.

Despite these measures, it's believed that personnel who come from socially deprived backgrounds are more likely to suffer further down the line, while events during deployment, such as being shot at, will also contribute to the variance.

Neil Greenberg, Professor in Military Psychiatry, KCMHR, said: 'The mental health needs of the UK Armed Forces are an important topic which is often the focus of media and political debate. This article provides an overview of the topic from both a historical and contemporary perspective. Importantly the article highlights some of the recent innovations that the UK military have introduced which are aimed at supporting the psychological health of troops and provides an overview of the wealth of research that had recently been carried out by King's College London in support of our military personnel.'

Professor Simon Wessely, Director of the KCMHR, said: 'If one simply followed the media reporting, especially the recent surge of "drama documentaries", one might be forgiven for thinking that there is an epidemic of mental health disorders in the British Armed Forces,

and that almost everyone who has served in either Iraq or Afghanistan is likely to end up mentally ill, homeless or in prison. The real research, reviewed in this paper, suggests this is not so. The rates of mental ill health have proven remarkably stable since 2003, generally better than the UK population as a whole, with the exception of alcohol misuse, which has been increasing. True, those who do have mental health problems continue to find it difficult to get help, but again, this is part of a much wider problem across society. And again, contrary to some views, the Armed Forces are aware of the mental health risks of modern warfare, and do take the issues seriously, even if simple solutions are not always available.'

> *It's believed that personnel who come from socially deprived backgrounds are more likely to suffer further down the line, while events during deployment, such as being shot at, will also contribute to the variance*

The paper is published today in a special issue of *Philosophical Transactions of the Royal Society B* which highlights recent advances in military casualty care.

The Royal Society is the UK's national academy of science. Founded in 1660, the Society has three roles: as a provider of independent scientific advice, as a learned Society, and as a funding agency. The Royal Society's expertise is embodied in the Fellowship, which is made up of the finest scientists from the UK and beyond. Their goals are to: invest in future scientific leaders and in innovation; influence policymaking with the best scientific advice; invigorate science and mathematics education; increase access to the best science internationally, and inspire an interest in the joy, wonder and excitement of scientific discovery.

13 December 2010

⇨ The above information is reprinted with kind permission from the Institute of Psychiatry, King's College London. Visit www.iop.kcl.ac.uk for more information.

© King's College London

UK charities struggle to cope with wounded soldiers

Information from Independent Catholic News.

By Pax Christi, Pat Gaffney and Tony Banks

The Army is putting too much pressure on charities by expecting them to care for 5,000 wounded troops, according to Tony Banks, an ex-paratrooper and campaigner for services charity Combat Stress.

'Until now, troops wounded in Afghanistan but medically unfit for service have been given desk jobs or light duties,' said Mr Banks, who served with 2 Para in the Falklands.

The MoD briefing paper leaked yesterday says that 5% of the Army's strength is no longer fit for combat. Inevitably, as the war in Afghanistan continues, that figure will increase but the Army has a responsibility for care for those men.

The MoD seems to be preparing itself for a media storm surrounding any attempt to discharge wounded servicemen.

Difficult decisions will inevitably need to be made about individuals who already have a significant media profile. These will require careful handling, writes Belinda Vern, a senior civil servant at UK Land Forces headquarters.

'Many of these men will also suffer from mental scars that have not had time to surface yet. On average it takes ex-servicemen 14 years before they approach Combat Stress for help. How do we know that charities will have enough money to care for these troops long term?' said Mr Banks, who is also MD of Balhousie Care Group.

General Sir Richard Dannatt, the ex-head of the Army, had promised that soldiers disabled in combat would stay with their units.

Mr Banks is currently working with the board of the Enemy Within appeal, which hopes to raise millions for Combat Stress.

Established in 1919, Combat Stress is the UK's leading military charity specialising in the care of veterans' mental health. Many of the conditions they treat are chronic and long-term in nature.

Pat Gaffney, General Secretary of Pax Christi, told ICN: 'This statement highlights what for the most part is a hidden cost of warfare, one that is rarely acknowledged: the physical and psychological toll on the servicemen and women. This is not just a cost of the moment... for many the consequences may be life-long and may also have a dramatic impact on family life and so the ongoing cost to society will be great. Those who make decisions about taking us to war have a responsibility for these decisions and the lives, both here and in Afghanistan and Iraq, that have been ruined by the wars.

'The 5,000 wounded troops mentioned in the statement are a reminder that we do not have "winners" in war and that there is no glory in war. War brings only losses... loss of life, loss of hope, loss of future opportunities..... in the words of Pope John Paul II, war is a failure of humanity.'

6 September 2010

⇨ The above information is reprinted with kind permission from Independent Catholic News. Visit www.indcatholicnews.com for more information.

Welcome

Goodbye

COMBAT STRESS

'Surgery saved my hand after bomb blast'

Private Neil McCallion was evacuated to the UK after suffering serious injuries in Afghanistan. He talks about the attack and rebuilding his life.

Private McCallion, 24, from Dunbartonshire, Scotland, wriggles the thumb and fingers of his left hand and shows how he can close them in a gentle grip. 'That's the most I've been able to move my fingers in ages,' he says. 'After the incident I thought they wouldn't be able to save my hand.'

The incident was a suicide bomb attack in Kabul on 4 September 2006, the day after his 22nd birthday. Private McCallion had been in Afghanistan for five weeks with the Argyll and Sutherland Highlanders. At 6am, a convoy set off to give water, stationery and clothes to schools.

'The kids were so excited to be getting stuff from us soldiers,' says Private McCallion. He and his friend, another private, were on top cover. This means they were standing in the lead vehicle, a Land Rover, and watching the roads. As the convoy left the second school of the day, Private McCallion felt a thud.

Cold and numb

'We skidded as a 4x4 vehicle came out of a side street and rammed into us. My friend shouted at it to get back as I turned and lifted my machine gun. The driver was looking right at me. Suddenly there was a loud droning noise and everything went black, then white. It felt like I was in a washing machine.'

The explosion blasted Private McCallion's Land Rover on to its side, dragging him along the road. He felt a cold numbness in his left hand. 'I saw a six-inch piece of metal sticking out of my hand. It was a mess,' he says. 'My index finger was hanging on by a wee white string, a tendon. I had to grab my hand and hold on to it.'

There was shouting and the smell of burning as he ran, dazed, into a side street, and collapsed.

'Everything was in slow motion,' he says. 'I opened my eyes and saw blue sky, and heard my sergeant shouting "Half pint!", which is my nickname on account of my size.' Private McCallion managed to get up and run to the convoy. As he did, he passed his friend's body on the ground.

With his own hand shattered and blood flowing from a shrapnel wound to his head, he thought he was going to die too.

Urgent medical care

Private McCallion was stabilised in a Kabul field hospital and flown to the UK that night, dosed with morphine and drifting in and out of sleep. 'I was worried about my friend. I knew he'd passed away and I couldn't stop thinking about him.'

In the UK, he went straight into surgery at Selly Oak Hospital in Birmingham, an NHS hospital with a special area for treating injured service personnel. Surgeon Garth Titley removed all the damaged bone, tissue and shrapnel from the hand, leaving it empty in preparation for repairing it.

When Private McCallion woke, his parents were by his bed. 'It was good to see them. I think they were relieved I wasn't more seriously injured,' he says.

Since then, he has had 14 operations, including one two weeks after the attack that used ribs, muscle and skin from his torso to rebuild his hand.

It was a shock when he saw the results. 'The back of my hand looked big, like there were ten burgers stacked up on it. I started crying and shouting that they might as well have taken my hand off. My mum ran out in tears.'

With encouragement from his surgeon and nurses, Private McCallion realised his hand would improve. Four weeks after his injury he managed to move a finger for the first time. It felt like a huge achievement. 'I called out to my parents that I'd done it. I was so excited. It was the next step towards recovery.'

Rehabilitation

Since then, a couple of setbacks have delayed Private McCallion's recovery by around 18 months. The ribs broke when he leant on his hand after his sixth operation, and a later fall snapped the titanium plates that were used to mend them. But with surgery and rehabilitation, including stretching elastic bands with his fingers, he is making good progress.

For five weeks in early 2009, his hand was temporarily attached by a flap of skin to his lower abdomen so that the blood supply could help regenerate skin on the back of his hand.

More operations are planned. Tendons will be removed from his leg and placed in his hand to allow him to straighten his fingers. Despite his restricted hand movement, he has passed his driving test and still walks his dogs when he's at home with his girlfriend in Dunbartonshire. He's looking forward to the day his hand is strong enough to go fishing again on Loch Lomond.

Private McCallion has had to cope with the psychological

as well as physical effects of the blast. In a split second, he lost a friend and the job he loved. He says regular sessions with a psychiatrist have helped a lot, allowing him to learn to feel safe. On his first trip to the shops, he felt sick and terrified. 'I was on red alert and thought I was back in Afghanistan,' he says. 'Now, I've got used to it and although I'm still on red alert sometimes, I can deal with it.'

As well as support from the military, NHS, family and friends, Private McCallion says contact with the battalion he left behind has really helped him. 'They sent me letters, parcels, jokes and sweets, and came to visit me when they could,' he says. 'I went to visit the battalion once when they were back here and it was brilliant. I've been away for two and a half years now and I really feel it. I'd go back tomorrow if I could.'

⇨ Reproduced by kind permission of the Department of Health – nhs.uk

Deaths in the UK regular Armed Forces

The latest National Statistic on deaths among the UK Armed Forces, produced by Defence Analytical Services and Advice (DASA), Ministry of Defence, was released on 31 March 2011 according to the arrangements approved by the UK Statistics Authority.

This National Statistical notice provides summary statistics on deaths in 2010 among the UK regular Armed Forces, and trends over the ten-year period, 2001–2010. This notice also presents information on comparisons to the UK general population. Previously published data on the number of incidents and cause of death have been updated from the latest information received from coroners.

Key points

⇨ In 2010, a total of 187 deaths occurred among the UK regular Armed Forces, of which 30 were serving in the Naval Service, 136 in the Army and 21 in the RAF.

⇨ In 2010, the overall mortality rate was 97 per 100,000, whilst in the Naval Service the rate was 78, the Army 116 and the RAF 49 per 100,000 strength.

⇨ During the ten-year period 2001–2010, the overall Armed Forces age and gender-standardised mortality rates fluctuated between a low of 70 per 100,000 in 2001 to a high of 107 per 100,000 in 2009.

⇨ The Naval Service mortality rate increased from 56 per 100,000 in 2009 to 78 per 100,000 in 2010. This was due to a rise in the number of deaths as a result of hostile action from seven in 2009 to 15 in 2010.

⇨ The Army mortality rate decreased from a high of 134 per 100,000 in 2009 to 116 per 100,000 in 2010, due to a decrease in the number of deaths as a result of hostile action from 99 in 2009 to 79 in 2010.

⇨ Overall, in 2010 there was no statistically significant difference in the occurrence of deaths in the UK Armed Forces compared to the UK general population.

⇨ In 2010, the Naval Service and RAF were at a significantly lower risk of dying compared to the UK population, whilst the Army were at a significantly increased risk of dying compared to the UK population.

⇨ In 2010, the cause-specific mortality rates for the regular Armed Forces were consistent with findings from the previous years:

↳ Hostile action was the single largest cause of death: 95 deaths (or 51% of total);

↳ Land transport accident deaths were the second largest cause (LTA): 36 deaths (or 19% of all deaths);

↳ Cancers accounted for 15 deaths (8% of the total);

↳ Other accidents accounted for 15 deaths (7% of all deaths);

↳ Suicides and open verdicts accounted for five deaths (or 3% of total).

⇨ In 2010, the UK Armed Forces were at an 80% significantly decreased risk of dying as a result of a disease-related condition compared to the UK general population.

⇨ In 2010, the UK Armed Forces were at a 94% significantly increased risk of dying as a result of external causes of injury and poisoning compared to the UK general population.

31 March 2011

⇨ The above information is reprinted with kind permission from the Office for National Statistics. Visit www.statistics.gov.uk for more information.

NHS CHOICES / OFFICE FOR NATIONAL STATISTICS

'I lost my leg in Iraq'

Information from NHS Choices.

Sergeant Mark Sutcliffe works at Selly Oak Hospital supporting injured military personnel. Three years ago he was a patient there himself when he lost a leg in Iraq.

Sergeant Sutcliffe, 29, from Peterborough, joined the army at 17, becoming a member of 2nd Battalion, The Royal Anglian Regiment, known as 'The Poachers' (part of the Desert Rats). He worked in Cyprus, Afghanistan, Northern Ireland and Sierra Leone and was then posted to Iraq in 2006.

After he lost his leg in combat, two goals helped him through the long months of recovery: 'I wanted to walk again and get back into uniform because they're the things I did before,' he says. With expert care and hard work, he has achieved both.

The incident

On July 18 2006, Sergeant Sutcliffe was on foot patrol in Basra when a rocket-propelled grenade (RPG) was fired at him. An RPG is an anti-armour weapon, primed to detonate on hard impact.

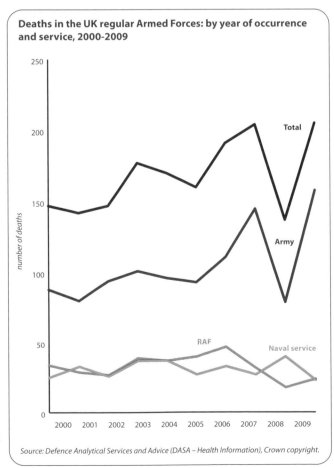

Deaths in the UK regular Armed Forces: by year of occurrence and service, 2000-2009

number of deaths

Total

Army

RAF

Naval service

2000 2001 2002 2003 2004 2005 2006 2007 2008 2009

Source: Defence Analytical Services and Advice (DASA – Health Information), Crown copyright.

'The RPG hit me directly in the back of the lower left leg and took the leg clean off,' says Sergeant Sutcliffe. 'Luckily, it didn't detonate. As I fell backwards on to the ground I saw my boot flying through the air with my foot, so I knew it had gone. The RPG carried on and unfortunately seriously injured an Iraqi boy.'

'I needed someone in uniform who I could relate to and have a laugh with; people who knew what I'd been through'

The troops scrambled to give Sergeant Sutcliffe morphine and apply a tourniquet. 'I remember seeing my sergeant stopping the bleeding with his hands before the tourniquet was put on. He saved my life,' says Sergeant Sutcliffe.

After three days in critical care at the field hospital in Iraq, he was evacuated to the UK.

On the ward

Sergeant Sutcliffe's arrival at Selly Oak Hospital, Birmingham, was the start of a four-month stay. 'My parents came into the ward shortly after I arrived and it was really good to have that first contact with them,' he says.

There were other injured service personnel on the ward, and a military liaison officer visited daily to make sure they and their families were looked after. 'The military presence on the ward was massively important,' says Sergeant Sutcliffe.

'I needed someone in uniform who I could relate to and have a laugh with; people who knew what I'd been through.'

Sergeant Sutcliffe had nine operations to save as much of his leg as possible. Dedicated care and support from the medical staff and from his family and friends helped him rebuild his physical and psychological health.

During his time in hospital, he experienced flashbacks and nightmares. He saw the attack as though it was on film. 'I would see the RPG hit me in the back and detonate on my body armour. I'd wake up screaming,' he says. 'It wasn't nice. But I was offered all the help I needed.'

After psychological assessments he was judged to be well. 'It's natural to have flashbacks and they started to subside,' he says. 'I don't have them at all now.'

Learning to walk again

In November 2006, Sergeant Sutcliffe moved to Headley

Court, a military rehabilitation centre in Surrey. Headley Court has a special limb-fitting centre where a prosthesis can be carved to fit a patient's stump almost perfectly.

Sergeant Sutcliffe's amputation is through the knee. 'Functionally, a through-the-knee amputation is better than above-the-knee because you've got a longer stump,' he explains. 'This gives you better walking ability and you can bear weight on it.'

With the physical challenges of surgery behind him, he put all his determination into walking again. At first it felt strange having a prosthesis. 'It was hard. You're learning to walk all over again and putting your trust in a piece of metal,' he says.

Despite this, Sergeant Sutcliffe achieved his goal of walking out of Headley Court for the Christmas holiday. 'I was on crutches and all over the place but I was walking,' he says. 'My parents had dropped me off in a wheelchair four weeks earlier, and the next time they saw me I was on my feet. It felt so good.'

Walking with a prosthesis is now second nature. 'I can't remember what it's like to walk with two legs.'

Swimming, skiing and back to work

Sergeant Sutcliffe spent four months at Headley Court, learning walking techniques and working hard at physiotherapy, such as swimming, to regain his fitness. Soon he progressed from two crutches to one. 'That's when I realised things were really going to get better,' he says.

By June 2007, nearly a year after his injury, he was able to walk without a walking stick.

Headley Court's limb-fitting centre offers top-of-the-range prostheses, and Sergeant Sutcliffe now has five: two walking legs, one running leg, one shower leg and one skiing leg.

'I'm still working on my running technique,' he says. 'I've been skiing twice to Colorado with the British Limbless Ex-Service Men's Association (BLESMA) and that was awesome. I fell over a lot and I'm not showing the same finesse I used to on the piste but I get down one way or another.'

He is now at ease with his prosthetic leg and is used to the attention he sometimes gets. 'I don't mind people looking because that's human nature,' he says.

'Kids make me laugh. I'll be pushing a trolley in the supermarket and a little kid will ask her mum why I've got a metal leg, and her mum will say "Shh!", but I don't mind. I'll show my leg to them. If I don't want to get attention, I wear long trousers not shorts.'

Sergeant Sutcliffe is still a proud Poacher but is now attached to Selly Oak as one of five military liaison officers. He asked to do the job, supporting injured soldiers and their families.

'The liaison officers assist injured soldiers through their recovery,' he says. 'Soldiers are making such sacrifices, and it's important we recognise that.'

⇨ Reproduced by kind permission of the Department of Health – nhs.uk

MoD completes review into women in close combat

An MOD press release.

The MoD has completed a review into the policy that excludes female members of the Armed Forces from carrying out ground close-combat roles and decided that it should remain unchanged. Women play an active part in front-line operations, undertaking crucial posts in areas such as logistics, artillery and engineering, but they cannot join the infantry or serve in small tactical combat arms teams where they are required to close with and kill the enemy face to face.

> **There is no question that some women would be able to meet the standard required of personnel performing in close-combat roles, both physically and psychologically. The key issue is the potential impact of having both men and women in small teams**

The policy was last reviewed in 2002 and the European Commission Equal Treatment Directive requires the UK to conduct a reassessment every eight years. Operations in Iraq and Afghanistan since 2002 meant there was considerably more evidence of women serving on the front line to be reviewed.

The study looked at recent literature on the effectiveness of mixed-gender teams in close-combat roles; the roles that women are undertaking in current operations; the experiences of both male and female military personnel who have served together on the front line, and evidence from other countries who have deployed women to close with and kill the enemy.

Minister for Defence Personnel, Welfare and Veterans, Andrew Robathan, said: 'The Service Chiefs and I all agree that women are fundamental to the operational effectiveness of Britain's Armed Forces, bringing talent and skills across the board. Their capability is not in doubt; they win the highest decorations for valour and demonstrate independence and initiative.

'We looked closely at the findings of this review but the conclusions were inconclusive. There was no evidence to show that a change in current policy would be beneficial or risk-free and so a decision was made to take a precautionary approach and maintain the current position.'

There is no question that some women would be able to meet the standard required of personnel performing in close-combat roles, both physically and psychologically. The key issue is the potential impact of having both men and women in small teams. Under the conditions of high-intensity close-quarter battle, team cohesion becomes of much greater importance, and failure can have far-reaching and grave consequences.

None of the research has answered the key question of the impact that gender mixing would have on the combat team in close-combat conditions. Accordingly, the MoD has decided that the case for lifting the current restrictions on women serving in close-combat teams has not been made.

The full report, including the research, has been published on the MOD website: http://www.mod.uk/DefenceInternet/AboutDefence/CorporatePublications/PersonnelPublications/EqualityandDiversity/Gender/WomenInCombat.htm

30 November 2010

⇨ The above information is reprinted with kind permission from the Ministry of Defence. Visit www.mod.uk for more information.

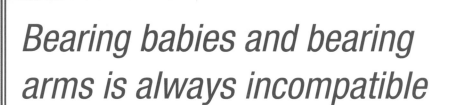

Bearing babies and bearing arms is always incompatible

Tilern DeBique didn't deserve compensation, but the whole discussion of women in the Army is ludicrous.

By Catherine Bennett

Like the right to box and the right to join the Garrick Club, the right to be Gordon Brown's cannon fodder is not one for which I have ever felt inclined to agitate. The death toll in Afghanistan and its unchanging accompaniment – Brown's routine about assaults upon civilians which would otherwise proceed directly from Helmand to Bloomsbury – only confirm that life is too precious to be placed at the disposal of Labour's armchair generals. The pressing question, surely, is not how do we get women into futile combat, but how do we keep men out of it?

The pressing question, surely, is not how do we get women into futile combat, but how do we keep men out of it?

But long before Brown and Blair reminded us of how cheaply the life of an 18-year-old is valued when political reputations are at stake, generations of women cherished the idea, however deluded and essentialist, that their sex was too peace-loving to fight. A sex difference this flattering is obviously hard to relinquish, even where the logic of equal rights demands it. In 2000, UN Security Council Resolution 1325 formalised what the Greenham women had always said: that male militarism must yield, ultimately, to female peacemaking. The resolution stated that women and girls suffered disproportionately in war and urged member states to involve women 'in all peacekeeping and peace-building measures'. Its demand for equal rights in conflict resolution was not matched, however, by a request that similar opportunities be offered to women in the preceding armed hostilities.

We might have relied upon that temple of undying conflict, Trevor Phillips's Equality and Human Rights Commission, to underline the dismally stereotyping nature of the UN approach. In a recent memorandum on the Armed Forces, EHRC officers recalled the anxiety of their predecessor regiment, the Equal Opportunities Commission, that 'societal attitudes' should not preclude consideration of 'women closing with and killing the enemy'. If the world has yet to produce a woman with sufficient bloodlust to command the EHRC, this body is keen to disseminate a more thoroughly martial approach, urging the Armed Forces to confront 'stereotypical views of the relative qualities of servicemen and servicewomen'. After some centuries of prejudice in this respect the Army has not done badly, you might think, in catching up. A few years ago, a pregnant soldier would have had to quit. Today, as we are reminded by the case of Miss, formerly Corporal, Tilern DeBique, the Army is happy to have single parents in its ranks as long as reliable childcare arrangements are combined with a willingness to make the ultimate sacrifice.

TONIGHT WE'LL READ HOW PRISCILLA'S LITTLE PONY INFILTRATES THE TERRORISTS' ORGANISATION.

It was not Miss DeBique's status as a single parent that led to her successful case for compensation – indignant Army message boards confirm that they are legion – but evidence that her superiors had not done enough to help her find childcare for Tahlia (now four), for reasons that were discriminatory. The Army's excuse that it had exempted her from weekend duties and early starts and, following her complaint, offered Miss DeBique a five-year posting with childcare, featuring a guarantee that she would not have to go to war (hardly a conventional understanding of readiness for combat), did not convince the tribunal.

It only emphasised the difficulties of sending a four-year-old's mother to war, even for the occasional afternoon, that Miss DeBique was obliged to take her daughter to the tribunal, where the child reportedly occupied herself with colouring books while her mother explained why she deserved around £1m in compensation for her losses, which included 'hurt feelings'. Confirming that the Army's requirement for soldiers to be available for duty '24/7, 365 days a year' was indirect sex discrimination (since women were more likely than men to be single parents with primary childcare responsibility), and that she should have been helped to recruit her sister from the Caribbean for help with childcare, the tribunal finally awarded DeBique a modest £17,016, including £2,016 for hurt feelings, a cause for much silent sorrow, no doubt, among employment lawyers who had earlier been crowing over a rich new seam of multiple discrimination.

Perhaps you have to be a lawyer to understand how an institutionally warlike organisation which requires from its employees a willingness to give their lives could ever conform with civilian expectations on fairness, let alone be expected to have their families' best interests at heart. What is the appropriate recruiting message: 'Happy kids make happy corpses!' perhaps? If the Army has been lamentably shortsighted in failing to anticipate the demands of single parents (particularly those recruited from abroad), then so, too, have equal rights campaigners who have agitated for an army that now requires a woman such as Miss DeBique to pledge her life in Britain's interests, when her death would leave a child effectively orphaned. The child of a military single mother must have some competing rights here that go beyond quality care while she is being sacrificed on behalf of President Karzai, who believes, *inter alia*, that women should have their husbands' permission to leave the house.

In practice, sex discrimination is already central to Army life: because of it, women soldiers, single parents or not, are less likely than male combatants to be killed, captured or maimed. To the frustration of anti-essentialist campaigners, the MoD is still exempted from parts of the Sex Discrimination Act, allowing the Army to keep women away – with many heroic exceptions – from close combat. Infuriating as this must be for female recruits who crave exactly this experience, there are probably many others who are quite satisfied with the exemption and, indeed, who envy DeBique her rejected no-war guarantee.

Among male soldiers as well as less fortunate female ones, one can conceive of a different response. When he was sentenced, in March, for going AWOL rather than having to return to Afghanistan, Joe Glenton was rebuked, more than anything, for letting his fellow soldiers down. 'Your absence,' said the judge advocate, 'meant that either your unit due to serve in Afghanistan was undermanned or someone else would have had to take your place.' Glenton is still serving a nine-month sentence.

A less extreme, but like-minded stringency about letting fellow soldiers down, by not turning up on parade, appears to have contributed to the sequence of events that led to DeBique's tribunal and subsequent pay-out.

The small award in her case, by a tribunal aware that any compensation would be compared to the sums paid for the missing limbs of Iraq and Afghanistan veterans, still fails to clarify the extent to which life in the Armed Forces should conform to civilian regulations. In particular, it muddies the question of single parents' duties in the Army. Should they be full participants, 24/7, in what an officer described to DeBique as a 'war fighting machine'? Or are they special cases, whose commitments are justifiably deputed to more flexible, more killable soldiers? Over to you, President Karzai.

18 April 2010

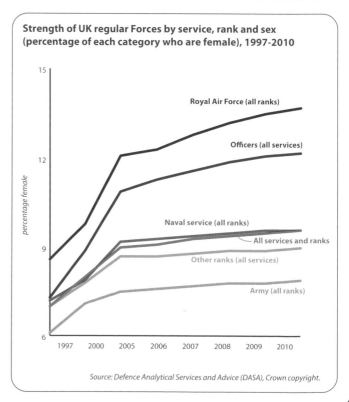

Strength of UK regular Forces by service, rank and sex (percentage of each category who are female), 1997-2010

Source: Defence Analytical Services and Advice (DASA), Crown copyright.

THE GUARDIAN

Catch 16–22

Recruitment and retention of minors in the British Armed Forces – introduction to a report from the Coalition to Stop the Use of Child Soldiers.

The UK is one of a handful of states – fewer than 20 – which still recruit 16-year-olds into their Armed Forces. The UK is isolated amongst its traditional military allies in this practice – no other country in the European Union and no other UN Security Council permanent member state recruits from this age. The few other states which do recruit at 16 include Iran, North Korea and Zimbabwe. Internationally, more than 130 states have set their minimum Armed Forces recruitment age at 18 or above, in line with the recommendations of expert international human rights bodies.

Children are not allowed to join the UK police or the fire service. They cannot watch 18-rated war films

The Armed Forces recruitment age is also anomalous at the national level. In the UK, legal majority is reached at the age of 18. Persons below this age are legally defined as children and are subject to special rights and restrictions. Notably, they cannot enter into legally binding contracts and there are specific restrictions on their employment in 'hazardous' work. Children are not allowed to join the UK police or the fire service. They cannot watch 18-rated war films.

In contrast, the Ministry of Defence deliberately targets young people for recruitment into the Armed Forces, resulting in large numbers of children being recruited each year. There are a number of legal and ethical questions concerning whether recruitment of under-18s strikes the right balance between offering educational and employment opportunities to young people, and the duty to protect them from possible harm while they develop their capacity to make informed decisions with far-reaching consequences.

The terms of recruitment and retention of young recruits[1] are problematic. Young recruits are bound by minimum periods of service which are longer than those imposed on adult recruits, under restrictive contracts which do not recognise the special legal status of children under national law. There is no ongoing right of discharge for under-18s and parents cannot withdraw their child from the Armed Forces after enlistment. It was recently revealed in Parliament that young recruits who attempted to leave the Armed Forces without permission have faced court martial and imprisonment in military correction centres.

The enlistment contract signed by 16-year-old recruits binds them into adulthood. This means that once they reach 18, recruits can be sent to the front line on the basis of an agreement they entered into while they were legally a child, without an opportunity to reconsider that commitment on reaching legal adulthood. This is a particular concern because the youngest recruits enlist in disproportionately large numbers to roles where the risk of death or serious injury upon deployment is up to 13 times higher than for other Armed Forces positions. There is an ethical question over whether someone so young should be allowed to make a contractual commitment with such serious consequences.

Evidence gathered for this report also indicates that young recruits are at greater risk of bullying, harassment and self-harm than older recruits. Recruits aged 20 and below[2] have significantly higher suicide rates than older colleagues. It has recently come to light that young recruits are also significantly more likely to drop out of training, resulting in tens of millions of pounds in wasted recruitment and training expenditure each year. Taken together, these findings call into question the ethics, legality, effectiveness and financial sense of maintaining the current minimum recruitment age.

In 2005, following the Blake Review into the deaths of several recruits at Deepcut Barracks in Surrey (two aged 17, one recently turned 18, one aged 20), the Defence Select Committee recommended that the Ministry of Defence examine the possibility of raising the minimum recruitment age to 18.[3] No such examination took place.[4] In 2008, the UN Committee on the Rights of the Child – the expert body responsible for monitoring states' compliance with international law relating to children and child soldiers – expressed concern at recruitment practices relating to under-18s in the UK and called for the minimum recruitment age to be raised to 18.[5] In 2009, this recommendation, and others relating to young people in the Armed Forces, was endorsed by Parliament's Joint Committee on Human Rights.[6] Despite these recommendations, the UK Government has not conducted a thorough review of the Armed Forces recruitment age for at least 100 years. Such a review is now long overdue.

The purpose of this report is to challenge the status quo currently surrounding the situation of young people in the UK Armed Forces today. It questions the ethics and legality of the restrictions on young recruits' rights of discharge, their minimum period of service, and their exposure to the risk of hostilities. The report also makes

COALITION TO STOP THE USE OF CHILD SOLDIERS

the case for a considered review and debate on the minimum recruitment age. It highlights the evidence that not only is the experience of recruits in the 16–18 age bracket adversely affected by their relative lack of maturity, but that their high drop-out rate results in millions of pounds in wasted expenditure.

Internationally, more than 130 states have set their minimum armed forces recruitment age at 18 or above, in line with the recommendations of expert international human rights bodies

The report concludes with recommendations to address these issues, focussing on the opportunity presented by the Armed Forces Bill currently before Parliament. The Coalition to Stop the Use of Child Soldiers calls on Parliament and the Ministry of Defence to:

⇨ Amend relevant regulations to replace the discretionary 'unhappy juniors' provision with ongoing discharge as of right for all existing recruits aged under 18 years;

⇨ Amend minimum terms of service for existing Army recruits who enlisted below the age of 18 to ensure they are equitable with terms of service for adult recruits (maximum of four years); and

⇨ Review the minimum Armed Forces recruitment age, with a view to raising it to 18 years.

Notes

1   The term 'young recruit' is used in this report to signify recruits aged below 18 years of age, unless specified otherwise.

2   Fully disaggregated data separating those aged below 18 is unavailable.

3   House of Commons Defence Committee (2005) *Duty of Care* (Third Report of Session 2004–2005), para.14.

4   Ministry of Defence, *The Government's response to the House of Commons Defence Committee's third report of session 2004-05, on Duty Of Care*, July 2005, para.14.

5   Committee on the Rights of the Child (2008) *Concluding observations on the initial report of the United Kingdom of Great Britain and Northern Ireland under the Optional Protocol on the involvement of children in armed conflict* (UN Doc: CRC/C/OPAC/GBR/CO/1), para.13.

6   House of Commons and House of Lords Joint Committee on Human Rights (2009) *Children's Rights* (Twenty-fifth Report of Session 2008-09), para.143.

March 2011

⇨ The above information is reprinted with kind permission from the Coalition to Stop the Use of Child Soldiers. Visit www.child-soldiers.org for more.

© Coalition to Stop the Use of Child Soldiers

Under-18s' right of discharge

Coalition to Stop the Use of Child Soldiers welcomes Ministry of Defence initiative on discharge for under-18s.

The Coalition to Stop the Use of Child Soldiers welcomes the announcement by the Minister for Defence Personnel, Welfare and Veterans that secondary legislation will shortly be introduced granting young Armed Forces recruits an ongoing right of discharge up until the age of 18 years. The reform was announced in the Government's response to the *Select Committee on Armed Forces Bill Special Report* on 19 May 2011.

The Coalition believes this new measure will create a much fairer system, end confusion, and provide an essential lawful route for unhappy young recruits to leave the Armed Forces. We welcome this initiative by the Ministry of Defence, which recognises the need to provide special legal protection to minors. It is also an important step towards implementing recommendations of the UN Committee on the Rights of the Child regarding the UK's compliance with the Optional Protocol to the Convention on the Rights of the Child on the involvement of children in armed conflict.

The Coalition also welcomes the recommendations made by Parliament's Joint Committee on Human Rights in its review of the Armed Forces Bill, published on 17 May 2011. Amongst its recommendations the Committee called for the minimum period of service for young Army recruits to be reduced, to end the current unfair disparity between adults and minors. The Committee also recommended Parliament use the Armed Forces Bill as an opportunity to reassess the use of under-18s in the Armed Forces. In this respect, the Coalition believed that the Armed Forces Bill offers an ideal opportunity to raise the UK's minimum recruitment age to 18 years, in line with recommendations of the UN Committee on the Rights of the Child and the practice of the majority of states worldwide.

May 2011

⇨ The above information is reprinted with kind permission from the Coalition to Stop the Use of Child Soldiers. Visit their website at www.child-soldiers.org for more information on this and other related topics.

© Coalition to Stop the Use of Child Soldiers

COALITION TO STOP THE USE OF CHILD SOLDIERS

Strategic Defence and Security Review published

The outcome of the Strategic Defence and Security Review (SDSR), which sets out how the Government will deliver the priorities identified in the National Security Strategy, has been published today, Tuesday 19 October 2010.

Securing Britain in an Age of Uncertainty: The Strategic Defence and Security Review details how our Armed Forces will be reshaped to tackle emerging and future threats.

There have been two main priorities in the review:

⇨ to ensure that our mission in Afghanistan is protected; and

⇨ to make sure we emerge with a coherent defence capability in 2020.

Afghanistan remains the MOD's top priority and we will do all we can to ensure success.

The SDSR aims to bring defence plans, commitments and resources into balance so that we have a coherent defence capability and a sustainable defence programme for the future

Defence cannot continue on an unaffordable footing. The SDSR aims to bring defence plans, commitments and resources into balance so that we have a coherent defence capability and a sustainable defence programme for the future.

Secretary of State for Defence Dr Liam Fox said:

'The front line has been protected because Afghanistan is the Government's top priority.

'Tough decisions are required to reconfigure our Armed Forces to confront future threats whilst we also tackle the £38bn deficit that has accumulated in the 12 years since the last Defence Review.

'The MOD must become as effective and as efficient as possible. Lord Levene will help me deliver radical reform to streamline the Department.'

The Permanent Secretary Sir Bill Jeffrey, and Chief of the Defence Staff Air Chief Marshal Sir Jock Stirrup, together with the service chiefs and other members of the Defence Board, have been closely involved throughout the review.

There will be some major changes to force elements of all three services to enable them to meet future force structures.

The review will lead to reductions in manpower over the next five years across all three services and the civilians in defence:

⇨ the Royal Navy will reduce by around 5,000 personnel;

⇨ the Army by 7,000;

⇨ the RAF by 5,000;

⇨ civilians by 25,000.

No changes will be made to front line Army, Royal Marine or RAF Regiment units while operations in Afghanistan continue.

Other impacts on the three services will include:

Royal Navy

The Royal Navy will have a number of capabilities, including the Trident Force, based around the four Vanguard Class submarines, one of which is always on patrol.

The Queen Elizabeth Class aircraft carrier will give the UK political and military flexibility in responding to crises. It will routinely have 12 Joint Strike Fighters, plus helicopters embarked for operations. The aircraft's 700-mile (1,100km) range over land and sea will enable it to carry out a broad range of missions.

The Royal Navy will be equipped with 19 frigates and destroyers to protect a naval task group and meet our standing commitments at home and overseas. These will include six new Type 45 destroyers and new Type 26 frigates.

This force, though smaller than currently, will provide military flexibility and choice across a variety of operations from full-scale warfare, through coercion and reassurance, to presence and maritime security (in particular protecting trade and energy supplies).

Seven new Astute Class submarines will contribute to the protection of our nuclear deterrent and naval task groups.

3 Commando Brigade will provide one element of our very high readiness response force.

The Royal Marines will be able to land and sustain a commando group by helicopter, and with protective vehicles, logistics, and command and control support from a specialist landing and command ship.

The Army will reduce by around 7,000 to about 95,000 personnel by 2015, but with no changes to combat units involved in Afghanistan, and an assumption, for now, of a requirement of about 94,000 by 2020

In order to meet this new structure the Royal Navy will:

⇨ reduce Royal Navy service personnel by around 5,000 to a total of about 30,000 by 2015, and with an assumption, for now, of a requirement of about 29,000 by 2020;

⇨ decommission HMS *Ark Royal* immediately;

⇨ decommission either the helicopter landing ship HMS *Ocean* or HMS *Illustrious* following a short study of which would provide the most effective helicopter platform capability, and place one landing and command ship at extended readiness;

⇨ decommission four frigates and a Bay Class amphibious support ship; and

⇨ rationalise the Royal Navy estate.

Army

The Army will be structured around five multi-role brigades, each including reconnaissance, armoured, mechanised and light infantry forces with supporting units of equipment and enablers. We will keep one brigade at high readiness available for an intervention operation and four in support to ensure our ability to sustain an enduring stabilisation operation.

The Army will retain 16 Air Assault Brigade, a high-readiness intervention brigade with supporting units, trained and equipped to be one of the first ground forces to intervene in a new conflict.

The Army will also retain the ability to command operations at very senior level through the UK-led Allied Rapid Reaction Corps (ARRC) headquarters (part of NATO). And we will retain our capacity to deliver one UK, fully deployable, senior level (divisional) headquarters, and the ability to regenerate a second deployable divisional headquarters.

In order to meet this new structure the Army will:

⇨ reduce by around 7,000 to about 95,000 personnel by 2015, but with no changes to combat units involved in Afghanistan, and an assumption, for now, of a requirement of about 94,000 by 2020;

⇨ reduce by one the number of deployable brigades, as we restructure to five multi-role brigades;

⇨ reduce our holdings of Challenger 2 tanks by around 40 per cent and our heavy artillery by around 35 per cent;

⇨ significantly reduce our non-deployable regional administrative structure; and

⇨ rationalise our deployable headquarters by reducing the communications and logistics support to Headquarters ARRC and convert the second of our operational divisional headquarters to a force preparation role.

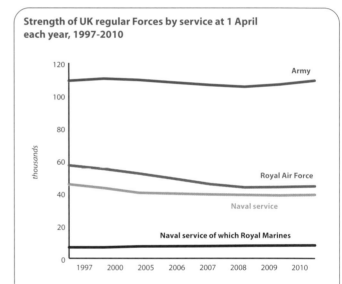

Strength of UK regular Forces by service at 1 April each year, 1997-2010

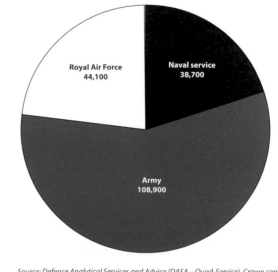

Strength of UK regular Forces by service at 1 April 2010

Royal Air Force 44,100
Naval service 38,700
Army 108,900

Source: Defence Analytical Services and Advice (DASA – Quad-Service). Crown copyright.

MINISTRY OF DEFENCE

Royal Air Force

The Royal Air Force's future capabilities will include a fleet of two of the most capable fast jets anywhere in the world: a modernised multi-role Typhoon fleet and the Joint Strike Fighter (JSF) to provide combat intelligence, surveillance, target acquisition and reconnaissance (ISTAR) capabilities.

It will also have strategic surveillance and intelligence platforms as part of our broader ISTAR capability, including: E-3D Sentry AWACS (Airborne Warning and Control System) to provide airborne command, control and surveillance; Rivet Joint signals intelligence aircraft to provide independent strategic intelligence gathering; and a range of remotely piloted air systems.

The air transport fleet will be upgraded with the addition of A400M transport aircraft and A330 future strategic tanker and transport aircraft as well as the planned C-17 fleet. These aircraft will enable us to deploy rapidly, support and recover UK forces and their equipment anywhere in the world, and provide airborne refuelling to maximise the range and endurance of our aircraft.

The support helicopter capability (both RAF and RN) will also provide battlefield mobility from land and sea, based on Chinook heavy- and Merlin medium-lift helicopters, able to move personnel and equipment rapidly over considerable distances.

In addition, RAF Regiment force protection squadrons at high readiness will protect deployed aircraft and personnel in hostile areas and provide elements of Defence's joint CBRN (chemical, biological, radiological and nuclear) detection capabilities.

In order to meet this new structure the Royal Air Force will:

⇨ reduce by around 5,000 personnel to about 33,000 by 2015, and with an assumption, for now, of a requirement of about 31,500 by 2020;

⇨ withdraw the C-130 Hercules transport fleet ten years earlier than planned as we transition to the more capable and larger A400M;

⇨ withdraw the Sentinel surveillance aircraft once it is no longer required to support operations in Afghanistan;

⇨ rationalise the RAF estate;

⇨ retain Tornados, which will continue to operate in Afghanistan;

⇨ remove Harrier from service in the transition to a future fast jet force of Typhoon and JSF. This will mean a gap for carrier fast jet operations. JSF, like Harrier, will be operated jointly by RAF and Royal Navy pilots;

⇨ not bring into service the Nimrod MRA4; and

⇨ withdraw VC-10 and the three variants of TriStar aircraft from 2013 as we transition towards the more capable A330 future strategic transport and tanker aircraft.

A study will be undertaken by the leadership of the regular forces and reserves into the future role and structure of the reserves. We expect this study to take about six months.

Changes on this scale cannot be managed by the usual manning regulators. A redundancy scheme will be run for service personnel and a paid early release scheme for civilians in accordance with the usual arrangements for such schemes, including – in the case of civilians – consultation with the trade unions.

Much effort will now be required to work through the detailed implications of the various SDSR decisions and their implementation.

Part of this will be the work of the Defence Reform Unit, which is looking at the organisation of MOD and will report in July 2011. This will ensure defence is delivered as effectively and efficiently as possible. Reforms will be implemented as the review progresses.

19 October 2010

⇨ The above information is reprinted with kind permission from the Ministry of Defence. Visit www.mod.uk for more information.

MINISTRY OF DEFENCE

The Strategic Defence and Security Review: a criticism

Alistair Thompson: the Strategic Defence and Security Review was not strategic and has not increased our security.

> **Alistair Thompson was Conservative candidate for West Bromwich East at the general election. He also runs Media Intelligence Partners with business partner Nick Wood, the former press secretary to Conservative leaders William Hague and Iain Duncan Smith.**

Today I will be attending the decommissioning ceremony of HMS *Ark Royal*. As this proud symbol of British maritime power is consigned to history I worry that we might have botched the Strategic Defence and Security Review, which could have consequences long into the future.

Last year, in an attempt to clear up the mess left by the previous Government, the Coalition undertook the SDSR. The Ministry's budget, under Labour stewardship, had been managed so disastrously that on an annual operating budget of about £13 billion, commitments on equipment and overspends totalled £36 billion, or nearly three years' worth of funding.

This could have possibly been justified if our Armed Forces were the best-equipped soldiers, sailors and airmen in the world, but they are not. Vital equipment was all too often simply not available to the men on the ground. While US soldiers travelled around in heavily-armoured trucks, our boys and girls had to make do with Snatch Land Rovers designed for the streets of Belfast, not IEDs in Helmand.

There has also been wide reporting of helicopter shortages, body armour and other items (that should have been in plentiful supply), forcing our troops to make do with what is available and sometimes relying on clothing sent from concerned family members. Is it any wonder that our US allies refer to the Army as 'the borrowers'?

And because of the political tinkering and interfering with projects, this has led to an average five-year delay of the in-service date of the equipment the MOD has ordered.

> *There has also been wide reporting of helicopter shortages, body armour and other items (that should have been in plentiful supply), forcing our troops to make do with what is available*

On top of these inherited problems the Government also wanted a reduction of eight per cent in the MOD's budget. Set against this backdrop the Government had a near impossible job of conducting our first SDSR for 13 years. Don't get me wrong, I had hoped that the resulting report would meet all of these competing demands, but it has not.

In broad terms the Government's policy agenda could be summed up by the phrase 'Advancing UK Interests' and in military terms this has two clear policy implications:

⇨ Defending current UK interests, territory, trade/goods and citizens. This could be defined as everything we do currently, or own.

⇨ Secondly a more proactive or even offensive capability, which allows our Government and Armed Forces to exploit opportunities. This in simple terms means having the ability to respond to situations and crises.

Suicide, open verdict and waiting verdict deaths by service and gender, 1984-2010, percentages

Legend: ■ Suicide □ Open ■ Waiting verdicts

Category	Suicide	Open	Waiting verdicts
All services – male	98%	97%	91%
All services – female	2%	3%	9%
Naval service – male	15%	22%	14%
Naval service – female	<1%	<1%	0%
Army – male	61%	55%	77%
Army – female	1%	2%	9%
RAF – male	22%	20%	0%
RAF – female	1%	0%	0%

Percentages have been rounded to the nearest whole number.

Source: Defence Analytical Services and Advice (DASA), Crown copyright.

CONSERVATIVEHOME

Our Armed Forces have always played important roles in both, which was why I was disappointed at a number of the proposed cuts which were announced. So let me explain why the current round of cuts have removed our ability in the short to medium term to carry out these two functions.

One of the most immediate and visual cuts was the loss of both the Invincible Class aircraft carriers and sea harriers that flew off of them. These allowed the UK to project its power, quickly fulfilling the second role of the military and in enough of a concentration to act as a deterrent to most nations fulfilling the primary role. And before this statement is dismissed by those cynics out there, we only have to look at their vital roles in recent conflicts, including those in the Middle East and their pivotal role in 1982 in the Falklands War.

Then there is the decision to axe Nimrod. To many unfamiliar with the work of these planes, their loss will mean little, but this aircraft has, in various forms, served with distinction since the early 1970s. It was originally designed to combat the threat of submarines from the USSR, but also had vital secondary roles of maritime surveillance and surface warfare.

More recently, the RAF has used the Nimrod R1 variant to gather 'electronic intelligence' through a vast array of classified gadgetry. This has allowed our forces to target and deal with enemy radar and missile sites and other key enemy electronic networks. This greatly speeds up that all-important goal of air superiority and its loss make us massively dependent on the US, or other NATO allies.

I will not write at length about the contract clauses which mean that we, the taxpayer, are going to spend a further

£200 million on not building the nine new nimrods the previous Government ordered. This is on top of the three and a half billion we have already spent on building them.

Finally, there are the cuts in the numbers of personnel. While I have no problems with cutting the numbers of pencil pushers flying desks in Whitehall, cutting the number of sailors, soldiers and airmen only stores up massive problems. Our forces are already over-stretched and until such time as the number of commitments are reduced we simply cannot cope with fewer personnel, unless when the next conflict happens, or a hurricane hits the Caribbean, we simply say 'not our problem'.

Do not get me wrong; I applaud some of the other elements of the SDSR, including greater resources to combat the threat of cyber-warfare and attack from an EMP, but some of these cuts seem to be driven by the Treasury and not by strategic need.

I do not mean to be overly critical of the Coalition as in many areas their work is vital, and the policies they are putting forward both progressive and radical. But I wonder if in hindsight the history books may well compare some of the decisions made in the SDSR with the decision to remove the Royal Navy's only presence in the Falklands in 1981. A decision that was as short-sighted as it was wrong.

22 January 2011

⇨ The above information is reprinted with kind permission from ConservativeHome, a website providing comprehensive coverage of Britain's Conservative party. Visit http://conservativehome.blogs.com for more.

© *ConservativeHome*

Looks like the military budget got cut again.

CONSERVATIVEHOME

It's time for Britain to merge its Army, Navy and Air Force

The top brass are guilty of putting their own interests ahead of those of the country, writes Con Coughlin.

In years to come, when our heirs reflect on the events that led to the merger of Britain's Armed Forces, they will identify Liam Fox's announcement this week of wide-ranging reforms to the Ministry of Defence's structure as the moment when the demolition of our proud military traditions began in earnest.

After decades of chronic under-funding, they will conclude, it was inevitable that a small country such as Britain could no longer afford the luxury of maintaining independent command structures for its Army, Navy and Air Force. With defence spending slashed from five per cent of GDP at the end of the Cold War to just two per cent by 2011, the individual services had already been reduced to such a parlous state that they could barely carry out even the most basic military tasks.

The evisceration of the Royal Navy's surface fleet meant that there were more admirals than ships for them to command. Drastic reductions to the numbers of combat aircraft had seen the Royal Air Force shrink to its smallest size since the First World War, to the point where unflattering comparisons were drawn with its equivalent in Belgium, a country not renowned for its aerial supremacy. And while the Army could claim to have retained a respectable number of combat brigades, it did not have the funds to equip them all.

Indeed, looked at from this perspective, it is easy to see why, rather than simply looking to streamline the command structure of the Armed Forces – as Dr Fox proposed this week – the next generation of politicians decided to go the whole hog and simply merge the three services into a single establishment.

This prediction might appear far-fetched, yet given the bold proposals that Dr Fox has set out, such an arrangement seems the logical destination. More to the point, the disastrous impact that years of inter-service squabbling has had on our defence capabilities suggests to many that the sooner such an amalgamation of our military resources takes place, the better.

It would, after all, solve a host of problems. Rather than the MoD being racked by petty in-fighting between the RAF and Royal Navy over which service will have responsibility for flying combat missions off the new multi-billion-pound aircraft carriers currently under construction at Rosyth, pilots would simply be drawn from Britain's unified air command. Similarly, the looming power struggle between the RAF and the Army over whether soldiers or airmen take the controls of the new generation of Apache attack helicopters would be neatly side-stepped.

The present Government would, of course, recoil from any suggestion that the aim of its proposed reforms is to follow the recent Canadian example of unifying the rival forces under a single command, and doing away with centuries of military tradition in the process.

Announcing his reforms this week, Dr Fox said that the main aim was to undertake a wide-ranging reform of the 'bloated and dysfunctional' Ministry of Defence, which, a full year after he assumed responsibility for the department, is still struggling to provide him with an accurate assessment of just how large its overspending really is.

Certainly, no one is going to quarrel with the Defence Secretary's determination to end the Ministry's long-

standing habit of indulging in 'fantasy' defence projects that are both unaffordable and undeliverable. These are the primary cause of the black hole in his department's finances, which is estimated at £36 billion, but might amount to billions more.

Yet a closer reading of the good doctor's prescription for healing these self-inflicted wounds suggests he is clearly of the opinion that it is the top brass that are mainly to blame, rather than the civil servants who are supposed to be running the MoD. This is demonstrated not least by his plan to remove the heads of the three services from the department's Defence Board – a clear indication that he sees them as ultimately responsible for the appalling cost over-runs.

With hindsight, it does seem remarkable that there was no ministerial representation on this key policy-making body, and that ministers had to wait until the service chiefs had concluded their deliberations before being informed of the outcome. Jim Murphy, the Shadow Defence Secretary, has admitted that the previous Government should have done more to bring the department into line, and that many of Dr Fox's reforms were long overdue.

But New Labour was never at ease with men in uniform – and given its unpopular involvement in the campaigns in Iraq and Afghanistan, was in no position to undertake such radical changes at the MoD. The fact that Dr Fox now seems determined to cut the military down to size, while bestowing greater powers on the civil servants who are equally culpable for the Ministry's profligacy, suggests that a significant shift is taking place in the balance of power within the defence establishment, one that is likely to have profound implications for the survival of the services as individual entities.

In future, the only serving officer on the reconfigured nine-member Defence Board will be the Chief of the Defence Staff, currently General Sir David Richards. This places an enormous amount of responsibility on the CDS's shoulders. As the representative of each of the Armed Forces, he will be expected to be fully informed on any issue relating to any of the services, a position that could place him at a distinct disadvantage when challenged by the well-briefed civil servants who will occupy the majority of the seats on the board. As one senior officer remarked yesterday: 'This is nothing short of a Civil Service takeover of the military.'

There will be those who see these changes as the Government's way of putting the uppity top brass back in their boxes after various injudicious comments on the limitations of Government policy on Libya and Afghanistan. Nor should it be forgotten that, having made much political capital from the public indiscretions of senior officers under Labour, the Tories are determined not to suffer similar indignities.

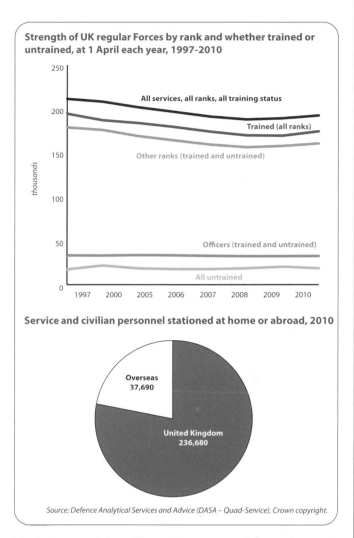

Strength of UK regular Forces by rank and whether trained or untrained, at 1 April each year, 1997-2010

All services, all ranks, all training status

Trained (all ranks)

Other ranks (trained and untrained)

Officers (trained and untrained)

All untrained

Service and civilian personnel stationed at home or abroad, 2010

Overseas
37,690

United Kingdom
236,680

Source: Defence Analytical Services and Advice (DASA – Quad-Service), Crown copyright.

Yet in terms of the military's long-term future, the really ominous development for the military chiefs is the proposed change to their command structure, which will involve a sharp reduction in the 'star count' – the number of expensive one-star officers and above – as well as a radical restructuring of the command chain. This will see the operational requirements of all three services brought under the control of a new Joint Forces Command, which will have overall responsibility for directing future military campaigns.

This lays the foundations for that future merger feared by those in the military. Yet, in many respects, the service chiefs have only themselves to blame. The bitter rivalries that erupted during last year's defence review undoubtedly had a detrimental effect on its outcome. Merging the Armed Forces into a single entity would not only put a stop to such counter-productive squabbling, it would provide us with the lean, mean fighting machine we will undoubtedly need to protect us against the many dangers that lie ahead. Our senior officers put self-interest above the national interest – and that is a luxury this nation can no longer afford.

29 June 2011

THE TELEGRAPH

Armed Forces Covenant
'an historic breakthrough'

The Royal British Legion today praised as 'an historic breakthrough' Prime Minister David Cameron's decision to write the principles of the Armed Forces Covenant into law.

'For the first time, Armed Forces personnel and their families will see the principles of fair treatment there on the statute book,' said Chris Simpkins, Director General of The Royal British Legion. 'Fairness for our brave Armed Forces can now be put to parliamentary scrutiny – an historic breakthrough that will benefit all those in service and their families for generations to come.'

He added: 'The Legion has campaigned vigorously for this and we applaud Mr Cameron for putting the Covenant principles in the heart of the new Armed Forces Bill, thereby fulfilling his promise made on HMS *Ark Royal* in June 2010 to write the Covenant into law.'

Following consultations with The Royal British Legion earlier this week, the Prime Minister, David Cameron, announced today that the Armed Forces Covenant would be written into law in a way that has the full support of The Royal British Legion.

'We are particularly pleased that the unique nature of service will now be acknowledged in the Bill, together with the principle that no disadvantage should arise from service – real issues for members of the Armed Forces. The inclusion of principles in the Bill will help Parliament to scrutinise the treatment the Armed Forces and their families receive,' said Mr Simpkins.

An annual review of the Armed Forces Covenant will be prepared by the Defence Secretary for Parliament under the independent scrutiny of members of an External Reference Group, which includes The Royal British Legion. Any criticisms by that group will be published – 'a satisfactory level of independent oversight,' said Mr Simpkins.

The Prime Minister also announced a Covenant support package which the Legion estimates to be in the range of £40 million to £50 million.

A new Armed Forces Community Covenant scheme will be introduced to support action by local communities to support Armed Forces and veterans.

A new Veteran's Card will be introduced, based on an expansion of the existing Defence Discount Directory scheme.

'The Royal British Legion stands ready to campaign on behalf of both these schemes, so that communities,

public bodies and the private sector will be provided opportunities to show their appreciation to our brave Armed Forces, veterans and their families,' said Mr Simpkins.

Greater support will also be given to those injured in service:

⇨ The Legion looks forward to Andrew Murrison's report that will ensure military amputees get access to prosthetics as good as the ones they are given at Headley Court, even after they leave the Armed Forces.

⇨ Seriously injured veterans and Armed Forces personnel will also be automatically eligible for concessionary bus travel across England.

⇨ Armed Forces personnel suffering genital injuries while on operations will get free access to three cycles of IVF treatment.

Families will also benefit from a new fund to support schools with a large number of pupils from Armed Forces families, while Council Tax relief will be increased from 25% to 50% for personnel serving on operations.

New powers will be introduced in the Ministry of Justice to improve the military inquest system.

'This is an impressive package of support, but even more impressive is the irrevocable legacy of at last getting the principles of the Armed Forces Covenant written into law. This is a major step forward for the whole Armed Forces community,' said Mr Simpkins.

'Credit is due not only to the Prime Minister, the Defence Secretary and other key ministers, but also to our supporters in Parliament – and especially to the crusading journalism of the *News of the World*, its readers, and the wider public, who have combined to deliver the best possible deal for our Armed Forces.'

15 May 2011

⇨ The above information is reprinted with kind permission from The Royal British Legion. Visit www. britishlegion.org.uk for more information on this and other related topics.

© *The Royal British Legion*

ROYAL BRITISH LEGION

The Armed Forces Covenant

The Government recognises the need do more to ensure our Armed Forces, veterans and their families have the support they need and are treated with the dignity they deserve.

The Military Covenant was conceived as an expression of the mutual obligations which exist between the nation, the Army and each individual soldier. It made clear that those who serve should expect to be treated fairly, to be valued and to be respected, in recognition of the extraordinary commitment and sacrifices which they were called upon to make.

The Government is rewriting the Covenant as a new tri-service document – the Armed Forces Covenant – which expresses the enduring, general principles that should govern the relationship between the nation, the Government and the Armed Forces community. This will set the tone for Government policy aimed at improving the support available for serving and former members of the Armed Forces, and the families which carry so much of the burden, especially in the event of injury or death.

> **The Military Covenant was conceived as an expression of the mutual obligations which exist between the nation, the Army and each individual soldier**

Concrete measures

We have already doubled the operational allowance for those serving in Afghanistan and ensured that their opportunities for rest and recuperation are maximised. We have also taken steps to ensure that those injured, either physically or mentally, receive the best possible care.

In the last month we have announced that we will provide further or higher education scholarships for children of service personnel who have died in the service of their country; enhancements to the scheme to enable service leavers to gain a first higher education qualification. This includes a 24-hour helpline which will provide counselling and support to veterans. In addition, the provision of healthcare to service personnel will be enhanced by an extra £20 million per year. This will pay for additional medical staff to deliver better mental healthcare facilities.

Earlier this year we also set up the independent Armed Forces Covenant Task Force led by Professor Hew Strachan to identify innovative answers to the most difficult problems facing serving and former service personnel and their families. The Task Force has examined, identified and assessed fresh ways of thinking about how the Government and society as a whole can fulfil its obligations to rebuild the Military Covenant and will report by mid-November.

> **Commitments and priorities (some of which have already been put into action):**
>
> ⇨ ensuring that service personnel's rest and recuperation leave can be maximised;
>
> ⇨ changing the rules so that service personnel only have to register once on the service voters' register;
>
> ⇨ exploring the potential for including service children as part of our proposals for a pupil premium;
>
> ⇨ providing university and further education scholarships for the children of servicemen and women who have been killed on active service since 1990;
>
> ⇨ providing support for ex-service personnel to study at university;
>
> ⇨ creating a new programme, 'Troops for Teachers', to recruit ex-service personnel into the teaching profession;
>
> ⇨ providing extra support for veteran mental health needs;
>
> ⇨ reviewing the rules governing the awarding of medals;
>
> ⇨ doubling the Operational Allowance;
>
> ⇨ including Armed Forces pay in our plans for a fair pay review;
>
> ⇨ ensuring that injured personnel are treated in dedicated military wards;
>
> ⇨ looking at whether there is scope to refurbish Armed Forces' accommodation from efficiencies within the Ministry of Defence.

May 2011

⇨ The above information is reprinted with kind permission from the Cabinet Office. Visit www.cabinetoffice.gov.uk for more information.

CABINET OFFICE

Some observations on the Armed Forces Covenant

By Joel Shenton, Editor, DefenceManagement.com

The UK now has a written tri-service Armed Forces Covenant. Defence Secretary Liam Fox has revealed a formal document, set out proposals for annual reports on the progress of the agreement itself and outlined a Covenant support package.

For many years the Covenant existed as an unwritten understanding between the nation and the Armed Forces, but now a document can be produced to be referenced, distributed and pored over by all. It is, as governments like to say, a step change in relations between the Government and Armed Forces.

It is not the detailed, legally binding covenant some had called for. Fox was clear that any such covenant could tie the Ministry of Defence up in European courts for years, but it is progress, and the Government must now endeavour to live up to it.

The document itself sets out the Government's obligation to service personnel and their families. 11 pages of text and diagrams give a broad outline of some of the key principles which had been assumed to be part of that obligation in the past.

'In the current financial climate we cannot do as much to honour that obligation [to forces personnel], or do it as quickly, as we would like, but we can make clear the road on which we are embarked,' Fox said at the Covenant's Parliamentary launch.

The report itself is not what was originally planned. The speedy and public announcement that the Covenant would effectively be 'enshrined' in law in the weekend before the announcement in Parliament followed a 90-minute meeting between Prime Minister David Cameron and Royal British Legion director general Chris Simpkins, who had previously been critical of the Government's plans.

> *Firstly, members of the Armed Forces community should not suffer disadvantage as a result of their service, and secondly, where appropriate, they should receive special treatment*

Cameron himself had promised a covenant 'written into the law of the land' in a speech given on HMS *Ark Royal* almost a year ago, but failed to back up the pledge in the text of the Armed Forces Bill.

Instead of writing the Covenant into law, the Government had initially promised an annual report on the Covenant produced by the Secretary of State for Defence alone. After widespread upset at the lack of external scrutiny, a U-turn was performed. The Government now, with all of an external reference group's comments published in the annual report, will be unable to hide from any failure to deliver.

The Covenant rests on two main principles, Fox said. Firstly, members of the Armed Forces community should not suffer disadvantage as a result of their service, and secondly, where appropriate, they should receive special treatment.

The new Covenant document and reporting promise, still to be discussed in the third reading of the Armed Forces Bill, are accompanied by a package of welfare measures set to cost around £50 million.

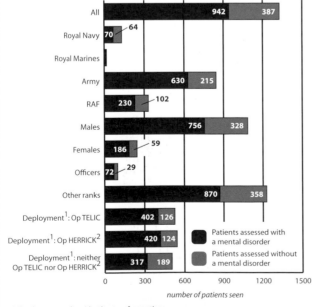

New episodes of care at the MoD's Departments of Community Mental Health (DCMH) by demographic and military characteristics, 1 July-30 September 2010, numbers

Legend:
- Patients assessed with a mental disorder
- Patients assessed without a mental disorder

Category	With mental disorder	Without mental disorder
All	942	387
Royal Navy	70	64
Royal Marines		
Army	630	215
RAF	230	102
Males	756	328
Females	186	59
Officers	72	29
Other ranks	870	358
Deployment[1]: Op TELIC	402	126
Deployment[1]: Op HERRICK[2]	420	124
Deployment[1]: neither Op TELIC nor Op HERRICK[2]	317	189

number of patients seen (axis: 0, 300, 600, 900, 1200, 1500)

1. Deployment to the wider theatre of operation.
2. Does not include personnel deployed to Afghanistan during period Jan 2003 to Sept 2005.

Source: Defence Analytical Services and Advice (DASA), Crown copyright.

Some of the measures were outlined in Professor Hew Strachan's Task Force report on the Covenant last year, although that report itself was dismissed as 'incredibly wet and feeble' by Forces Pension Society chairman Vice-Admiral Sir Michael Moore.

Regardless, Professor Strachan's community Covenant recommendations were included along with a pledge for £30 million of funding until 2015 to support 'joint projects, at a local level, between the services or veterans groups and the wider community'.

Council tax relief for personnel serving on operations will be doubled to 50 per cent, and a fund of £3 million per year over and above the existing pupil premium will go to help support state schools catering for significant numbers of service children.

Veterans will be entitled to a card which, while it will not act as a form of identification, will give them access to commercial discounts and privileges.

Also, veterans who have suffered serious genital injuries in service will have access to three cycles of IVF wherever they live.

Future reports on prosthetics and housing were also promised.

The Government has already doubled the Operational Allowance for service personnel, although this does not, as has recently been shown, apply to pilots flying over Libya. It has also brought in scholarships for the children of bereaved service families.

While a cynic might point out that welfare measures are the least costly improvements to make, there is no doubt they are welcome and, some would argue, overdue, but this is clearly just the beginning of the Covenant journey.

Were the terms of employment and remuneration believed to have been in the unwritten Covenant? They don't appear to have made it into the written document.

Lord West, the former First Sea Lord, has said that the success of the Covenant must 'not be used as a smokescreen to cover the fact that we are cutting the military to the bone'.

Armed Forces personnel are still subject to an ongoing pay freeze, and while the Government has boosted pay for the lowest-paid personnel, recent cuts of £250 million from allowances – including Continuity of Education Allowance – could leave some personnel and their families aggrieved.

There is still no recourse for military personnel angered by changes in pension indexation from the Retail Price Index to the generally lower Consumer Price Index – a move which could cost service personnel thousands of pounds over their lifetime.

As with many Government decisions, the 'financial climate' is said to loom large in the decision-making process. Until that improves, this is a document and commitment to be welcomed by all.

18 May 2011

⇨ The above information is reprinted with kind permission from DefenceManagement.com. Visit www.defencemanagement.com for more information.

© DefenceManagement.com

Yes, we owe our Armed Forces – but Cameron's leaky law is not enough

Cameron's promise of a legally binding 'military covenant' means little if spending cuts and ill-advised wars continue.

By Jackie Ashley

There's a great British tradition of cheering on the troops at war, and then treating them abominably when it's over. Heroes today, forgotten tomorrow. Go back to drawings of Crimean veterans, or the mutilated victims of the trenches doing menial jobs to survive, or, more recently, alcoholics in hostels, now unrecognisable as khaki-uniformed 'heroes'.

Ever since we've had a professional army it has attracted young men, often barely more than boys, who are running from bad homes or a shortage of jobs. They get comradeship, discipline, sometimes bullying, but at any rate a purpose and a structure. Then one day, they have done their time and are pushed back into a civilian world they find alien and aren't equipped to handle.

That's a historic picture, of course, and a lot has changed. Some of it for the better: the Ministry of Defence spends more time and money trying to prepare troops for jobs outside the forces. There are world-class British surgeons and specialists waiting for the most seriously injured cases.

But the bigger changes have been for the worse. The Iraq war, followed by increasing doubts over Afghanistan, means there has not been the 100% public support soldiers might expect. Recent fighting has been nearer to the experience of Suez, when British troops had to do their job in the knowledge that some back home were unsure about the whole thing. That must be hard.

Add to that the hammering the Armed Forces are taking in the Coalition cuts, with David Cameron himself acknowledging that there will be 11,000 redundancies, possibly including troops now on the front line in Afghanistan. Some 2,700 are to go from the RAF, where fighter trainees on the verge of getting their 'wings' were recently told they weren't needed. The price the Navy is paying for its two big new carriers is the lack of enough aircraft to put on them, and 3,300 lost jobs.

That's the background to the announcement on Sunday about giving legal status to the 'Military Covenant'. Broadly speaking, the Covenant states that in return for being willing to die for their country, members of the Armed Services have a special right to housing, healthcare, decent pay and education for their children.

Put like that – and who could be against it? – Cameron says simply: 'we owe them'. The Royal British Legion, allied with the *News of the World*, has fought a powerful and emotive campaign. Jim Murphy, Labour's impressive and plain-speaking defence spokesman, who has campaigned for ages for this, criticises only the fact that the Government has had to be pushed into it.

Yet there are some obvious questions. Eagle-eyed readers may have spotted that decent pay, welfare, housing and the rest of it are things that most Britons still living in a welfare state thought they were already supposed to get. Are we now saying that the general level of, for instance, education, is so low that families from the Armed Forces have to be airlifted out, and given special treatment? Soldiers who have experienced psychological or physical trauma certainly need specialist care. But what are we saying about traumatised victims of other situations, and the wider mental health needs of the country? Are we accepting that good care is now so rare it has to be rationed?

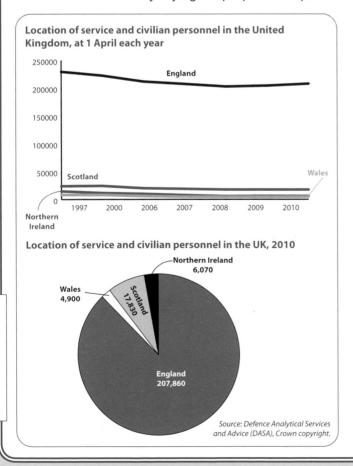

Location of service and civilian personnel in the United Kingdom, at 1 April each year

Location of service and civilian personnel in the UK, 2010

Northern Ireland 6,070

Wales 4,900

Scotland 17,830

England 207,860

Source: Defence Analytical Services and Advice (DASA), Crown copyright.

A second issue is that the decisions the Coalition has already taken seem to undercut the spirit of the Covenant it now wishes to make the law of the land. Making service people redundant hardly suggests they are valued. By changing the measure of inflation used to calculate pensions, including people serving in the forces now, and war widows, ministers are cutting the money they'll get. According to Jim Murphy, a 28-year-old corporal who lost both legs would lose £587,000 by the time he is 70 and the widow of a staff sergeant killed in Afghanistan would lose almost £750,000 during her lifetime.

There's a great British tradition of cheering on the troops at war, and then treating them abominably when it's over. Heroes today, forgotten tomorrow

Will such decisions be open to legal challenge? Will ex-soldiers be able to take the Ministry of Defence to court if they feel they have not been properly prepared for civilian life? The Defence Secretary, Liam Fox, made clear on Sunday this will not be the case, in which case the whole exercise may be no more than the kind of vapid headline-pleaser and newspaper-tickler that gave New Labour such a bad name.

But I think there is an even bigger question, which is what we actually want our armed services to do. The Iraq war was bad not just for the soldiers but for the politicians who sent them there: the 'Military Covenant' was an act of embarrassed contrition. Today, however brave and militarily successful individual actions are in Afghanistan, hardly anyone believes there can be 'victory' there.

One day we will talk to the Taliban. One day, perhaps soon, we will pull back to bases and then start to leave, and the Taliban will return. Maybe the threat of revived terrorist camps and plotting in Afghanistan and northern Pakistan will be damped down by drone attacks. But it will be a long way from the rebuilt, democratised and vaguely liberal Afghanistan the starry-eyed idealists told us would emerge from the gunfire. More soldiers, more gunships, can win more weekly battles. But is successful nation-building really on the table? Is there the political will left in austerity Britain, or debt-challenged Washington?

I doubt it. If so, and if the Taliban return, what are the politicians going to say to the wounded veterans and the widows and orphans of the soldiers who are fighting there now? The question hangs over the Military Covenant like a pall of grimy smoke.

Today the Commons has a chance to debate 'the Middle East, north Africa, Afghanistan and Pakistan'

– a huge agenda with many unanswered questions. What's needed is a clear explanation of the future of the Afghan war and the Coalition's thoughts on the conditions needed for future engagement.

We are teetering still on the brink of a deeper thrust into the Libyan conflict; but despite enthusiasm at the top of the military and in Whitehall about intensifying efforts there, the chances of state-building in Libya are hardly any higher than in Afghanistan. So how long are we prepared to stay involved in Libya? We are not the world's police force and we cannot afford to pretend we are. We should cancel the Trident replacement and refashion our forces for the more modest and genuinely defensive roles they can play.

Then we should certainly look after them properly, with good equipment, pensions and homes. I fear that a piece of flimsy, leaky legislation aimed at pleasing newspaper editors is no substitute at all.

15 May 2011

THE GUARDIAN

What is the Territorial Army (TA)?

Territorial soldiers and officers train in their spare time to provide support to full-time regular units when they're needed. When the Army goes on operations overseas, you'll find Territorial soldiers serving alongside the Regulars. From doctors and nurses in field hospitals to infantry soldiers working on the front line, most Army jobs are open to Territorials.

Regional or National?

There are two types of Territorial Unit – Regional and National. Regional Units train on week nights and some weekends and recruit from the local area. You don't need specific skills to join as you get all the training you need. National Units tend to be more specialised and recruit people with relevant experience from all over the country. Because members travel further to get to training, they don't train on week nights.

Territorial training

All the training for your Army job takes place in your spare time, with evening and weekend training sessions and short residential courses. Once you've got the skills you need to do the job you'll attend regular sessions with your unit. If you meet your minimum commitment by training for 27 days in a year with a Regional Unit, or 19 days with a National Unit, you get a tax-free cash bonus.

From bricklayers who use their skills to build Army bases to IT professionals who help set up military communications networks, you'll find a wide range of people doing a wide range of jobs

Who joins us?

People from every walk of life serve as Territorials. From bricklayers who use their skills to build Army bases to IT professionals who help set up military communications networks, you'll find a wide range of people doing a wide range of jobs. But you don't have to choose one that matches what you do in civilian life – many people take the opportunity to learn a completely different skill.

Professionally qualified?

If you've got certain professional skills and qualifications from your civilian career, you can put them to good use as a Territorial. You could be a construction engineer wanting to put your skills to the ultimate test, or a doctor looking to expand on NHS experience. Whatever skills you have, the TA is a great way to use them in a different context. Visit your local Army Careers Information Office to find out more.

Get paid to train

Territorials are paid to train, and get subsidised food and travel. It's a great way to earn some extra cash.

Training and skills

You can choose a job that develops your skills, or learn new ones – and everyone gets the same military training.

The joining process

When you apply to become a Territorial, you get expert help to find the Army job that's right for you.

⇨ The above information is reprinted with kind permission from the British Army. Visit www.army.mod.uk for more information.

© Crown copyright

Leaving the Armed Forces

Every year, 24,000 people leave the Armed Forces. If you're planning to be one of them, take advice from someone who's already made the move.

'I made the decision to leave the army because of a number of factors,' explains 27-year-old Rob, a former Captain in the British Army. 'I realised it wasn't something I wanted to do as a long-term career, due to time away on operational tours. Then I worked out that if I didn't want to make a career out of it, I needed to get out while I was still young enough to start something else.'

Rob says the biggest challenge facing anyone leaving the Army, Navy or RAF is the massive change in lifestyle.

'You're going to an environment where everyone may be supportive and want to help people in your position – people who've fought for their country – but ultimately very few of them will understand where you're coming from, what kind of experience you've got and therefore what you are capable of,' he explains.

Budgeting off barracks

The other big problem is more straightforward: money and all those bills and bits of paper you didn't need to worry about while you were serving.

'The Armed Forces cover just about everything,' says Rob. 'If you have a bit of a big session on the first day of the month and run out of cash, you can just lock yourself inside the camp, take on extra duties and wait for payday to come round without too much trouble. Outside, that doesn't apply. You have to make sure you can cover your basic bills.'

Rob says you need to consider the following expenses when you're deciding what kind of job to get and where you want to live:

⇨ Council tax;

⇨ National insurance;

⇨ Rent payments;

⇨ Bills like gas, electricity and Internet.

Getting support on Civvy Street

Fortunately, there are plenty of organisations who can assist if you find you need help with retraining, career advice, finding a home or paying bills. Steven Williams, an advisor with SSAFA Forces Help, suggests the following:

⇨ www.civvystreet.org.uk – for practical advice on completing a CV and helping you translate the skills you already have into civilian-speak, and for grants to help with retraining and vocational courses.

⇨ The Regular Forces Employment Association – has regional employment consultants, so you can see someone locally.

THESITE.ORG

⇨ The Career Transition Partnership – you should hear about this through your unit welfare officer when you make your decision to leave.

Finding a civilian job

The Ministry of Defence says 96% of ex-Armed Forces employees are re-employed within six months, but Rob believes many former servicemen and women don't get the job they want because they find it hard to explain to employers how their military experience is relevant to a civilian job.

'In the Army, everything's decided by rank structure,' he explains. 'Outside the Army, your career depends on qualifications, skills and experience. Most soldiers leave with good experience, and stronger skills than they might realise. Often, the only thing they need to work on is education.'

Rob left the Army without a degree, but still managed to get a job he's proud of. 'If you show a work ethic, show that you're proactive – for example, doing civilian work placements to gain experience before you leave the Army – then you will be able to get round any holes in your CV.'

AWOL isn't the answer

Both Rob and Steven say the most important thing is to plan in advance – don't just get up one day and decide you're quitting. You're likely to get more sympathy and support from your Commanding Officer if you come up with a concrete plan of action. 'The earlier you can start the transition, the better,' says Rob. 'The minute you have any kind of doubt about wanting to continue, you should start thinking about what you would do if you were to leave. Start spending as much time in a civilian environment as possible.'

Feeling overwhelmed by stress, and not having a plan for life after the Armed Services, can lead to feelings of desperation and result in individuals going AWOL (**A**bsent **W**ith **O**ut **L**eave). But don't give up hope: there is support for you. SSAFA offers a confidential support line on 0800 731 4880. If you find yourself considering this option, Steven Williams urges you to consider the potential repercussions: 'You may have difficulties accessing benefits and using your National Insurance number to gain employment. The longer you're AWOL, the worse you're going to feel, but it's not necessarily as bad as you may think.'

Updated 4 October 2010

⇨ Original article from www.thesite.org, a UK website supporting 16- to 25-year-olds, run by online charity YouthNet. Information was correct at time of print and written for a UK audience. Reproduced with permission.

Ex-military to be inspiring role models for young people

Information from the Department for Education and Skills.

Former members of the Armed Forces will become mentors to young people in schools across England following a £1.5 million grant to the charity SkillForce, Education Secretary Michael Gove announced today.

Through three pilot programmes, ex-service personnel will be fast-tracked into schools, using the skills and experience gained on the front line to help young people achieve. SkillForce will be funded to set up the three programmes from September 2011:

⇨ Military to Mentors: 100 ex-service personnel will be trained to work as mentors for young people in and out of schools across England. SkillForce will work alongside two other organisations, Endeavour and the Knowsley Skills Academy, on this programme.

⇨ Zero Exclusion Pilot: SkillForce will provide intensive support to 100 young people at risk of exclusion from school. This will take place in five regions across England (areas to be confirmed), over a 12-month period.

⇨ Expand SkillForce Core Programme: investing in the existing SkillForce programme that uses teams of instructors from military backgrounds to work with disadvantaged young people, helping them gain qualifications. Over a year, the charity will support 340 additional young people from parts of the country with high unemployment and deprivation. Part of this will include elements of the Zero Exclusion pilot.

These schemes are part of the Government's broader drive to encourage Armed Forces leavers to use their talents to help raise standards in schools. The move is inspired by a similar, highly successful programme in the United States.

28 February 2011

⇨ The above information is reprinted with kind permission from the Department for Education and Skills. Please visit their website at www.education.gov.uk for more information.

THESITE.ORG / DEPARTMENT FOR EDUCATION AND SKILLS

Veterans' mental health

The Mental Health Foundation recognises the importance of appropriate and timely mental health support for people who have served in the Armed Forces.

To achieve this, the following points are critical to the commissioning and provision of services.

⇨ Commissioners and providers of services need to provide a full range of appropriate and evidence-based interventions for a range of disorders, including depression, PTSD and treatment for alcohol and/or drug misuse.

⇨ Veterans could be encouraged to seek help if there was a better understanding, among primary health care and social care professionals in particular, of the culture of the Armed Forces, the particular pressures that veterans may be under and the risk of veterans developing mental health problems. There is a strong case for veterans to be involved in awareness training for health and social care professionals who come into regular contact with veterans.

⇨ Veterans themselves need to recognise that seeking help for a mental health issue is not a sign of weakness. Local mental health promotion initiatives could usefully include veterans as a specific target audience. There is an equally strong case for veterans to be involved in providing peer advice, advocacy and support to other veterans who may be at risk, or have an identified mental health need.

⇨ Given the number of veterans who are either within the criminal justice system (especially in prison, where there are known to be very high levels of mental health problems) or experiencing homelessness or problems with housing, more research is needed into the factors that prevent some veterans from returning to civilian life successfully, so that these can be tackled as a matter of priority.

⇨ Two cohorts appear to be at particularly high risk of developing mental health problems: younger veterans with a relatively short period of service (early service leavers), and reservists who have served in combat zones. Planners and commissioners of services need to take this into account when considering the needs of their local populations, and where resources (including specialist outreach services) need to be targeted.

⇨ Some veterans, such as those leaving the Armed Forces after a relatively short period of time and younger veterans, receive abbreviated support from the Ministry of Defence in terms of preparing them for the transition from the services to civilian life. The Ministry of Defence should consider how this support can be enhanced so that it reflects existing and likely future need rather than just length of service.

⇨ The 2003 review of support available for veterans (Dandeker, 2003) made a number of policy suggestions relating to in-service initiatives, transitional arrangements between service life and civilian life, and post-service life, including enhanced mental health service support and more flexible provision of housing. A number of these have seen good progress over the past few years but the Ministry of Defence and Department of Health should carry out an audit on these suggestions, and commit to action where progress has been slow.

Background

Overall, levels of mental health problems among veterans are not significantly different to those within the general population. However, a significant number of veterans do experience high levels of mental health problems, ranging through anxiety, depression and post-traumatic stress disorder and sometimes involving alcohol and drug misuse. Many do not access services that might be able to help them.

For some veterans, mental health problems arise many years after they have left the services, but may be related to experiences they had in the services. Frequently, the culture of the Armed Forces results in veterans showing a reluctance to attribute their condition to their service.

The incidence of mental health issues arising from military service is a major issue; since 2005, for example, Combat Stress has reported an increase of 72 per cent in the number of former military personnel seeking help. Their current workload includes over 4,400 veterans.

The Government has recognised this issue, and, commissioned the *Fighting Fit: a mental health plan for servicemen and veterans* report by Dr Andrew Murrison MP, which was published in October 2010. The report's

MENTAL HEALTH FOUNDATION

four main conclusions included provision of a trialled online early intervention service, a veterans' information service, an increase in the number of mental health professionals conducting veterans' outreach work and an inquiry into current mental examinations for serving members of the Armed Forces. In response, the Secretary of State for Defence, Dr Liam Fox MP, announced that the Government would introduce a dedicated 24-hour support line for veterans, and the introduction of 30 dedicated mental health nurses to ensure that the right support is available specifically for veterans.

1 February 2011

⇨ The above information is reprinted with kind permission from the Mental Health Foundation. Visit www.mentalhealth.org.uk for more information.

© *Mental Health Foundation*

MoD offers PTSD therapy

The Ministry of Defence (MoD) has revealed that it is to offer post traumatic stress disorder therapy to help service personnel, with Eye Movement Desensitisation and Reprocessing (EMDR) and Cognitive Behavioural Therapy both available.

Dr Robin Logie, a Clinical Psychologist and President of the EMDR Association UK and Ireland, admitted he had misgivings about the treatment before he trained in it.

But Jane Steare, mother of murdered British woman Lucie Blackman, stated that EMDR has helped her come to terms with the loss of her daughter.

Speaking to BBC News, she explained that prior to the therapy, she had been unable to stop imagining how Lucie was killed.

'I just kept thinking about it and I couldn't stop thinking about it. If it hadn't been for EMDR I think I would have gone totally, totally mad,' she said.

Dr Peter Martin, a Chartered Counselling Psychologist, said: 'The use of EMDR by the MoD is to be welcomed. As a Counselling Psychologist, I have used this method in an integrated therapy with motorcycle and other road traffic accident victims effectively now for over a year.

'Counselling Psychology is a broad church which is able to encompass newer ways of responding to distress having critiqued their claims and in the context of wide experience.

'There is a scientific basis for this kind of work and it is the job of the well-trained therapist to inform the potential client of this before consent for treatment is gained.

'I did part of my EMDR training partnered by an MoD therapist. The method's "No nonsense, just provide a safe container for the client to work out their own internal solution" seemed to suit the semi-closed world of the military.

'May fewer veterans suffer as a result of this brave move!'

The Division of Counselling Psychology will be holding their Annual Conference from the 12-14 July [2011] at the Thistle Grand Hotel in Bristol.

We're really pleased to have feedback on this news **item and have the opportunity to ensure that the facts of this story are fully accurate. Since we published this story we have received the following clarification from two members of our Society.**

⇨ Dr Wendy Frappell-Cooke CPsychol MBPsS: Defence Clinical Psychology Service, Joint Medical Command

⇨ Dr Jamie Hacker Hughes CPsychol CSci FBPsS: Head of Defence Clinical Psychology Service, Joint Medical Command

We should like to clarify what has been posted on the BPS website and included in the recent Division of Counselling Psychology newsletter where it is stated that 'the Ministry of Defence (MoD) has revealed that it is to offer post traumatic stress disorder (PTSD) treatment using Eye Movement Desensitisation and Reprocessing (EMDR) and Cognitive Behavioural Therapy (CBT)'.

In fact, both EMDR and CBT have been offered within the MoD as treatments for PTSD and other psychological problems for many years by members of all groups of mental health professionals within the Defence Mental Health Services. The MoD now employs, amongst others, four clinical psychologists and community mental health nurses who are EMDR consultants, several other psychologists, psychiatrists and mental health nurses who are eligible for practitioner status in EMDR and many others who are trained and working towards EMDR practitioner status.

In respect of CBT, the MoD employs a number of Psychologists, mental health nurses and psychiatrists who are accredited CBT therapists and many others who are trained and working towards this status.

The Defence Clinical Psychology Service provides a psychology service for military personnel as part of Defence Mental Health Services and the provision of therapy is regularly monitored and updated. The MoD takes seriously the mental health and wellbeing of service personnel and consequently provides, and has provided for many years, evidence-based therapies as recommended by NICE guidelines.

9 June 2011

© *British Psychological Society: www.bps.org.uk*

Veterans and homelessness

Case studies from Veterans Aid.

These stories are true; they are about real people. Some have left behind the problems that brought them to Veterans Aid (VA) and have asked that we share their experiences but not their identities. Their names are bracketed by commas.

Others have agreed to be named and identified. Every story is different, every tragedy unique, but VA's philosophy is a positive one.

CEO Hugh Milroy says: 'Most people make the transition from service to civilian life with no problem; they don't become homeless and they don't need further support. Others, through a combination of circumstances, and through no fault of their own, need help. That's why we're here.

'Our message is "Don't wait until you're desperate"; we'd rather speak to people before they get into serious difficulties. Our core business is homelessness, but our expertise, understanding and linkages with other support agencies make us a gateway for help with a wide range of problems.'

'Fred'

'Fred ' is a bright, dapper man with a twinkle in his eye and a treasure-chest of stories to tell. He's also 86 years old and, until recently, alone in the world.

When he arrived back in England after years living overseas the former Marine had only one ambition: to spend his remaining years in the country of his birth.

Without family, friends or anywhere to stay, 'Fred' arrived at Heathrow tired and without a clear plan. He was directed to London's Victory Services Club by a helpful airport information worker. It was a good call, because in a way 'Fred' did have a family – he just didn't know it.

Every former serviceman and woman has access to support agencies and friends; their needs may differ, but without a place to live other requirements pale into insignificance. 'Fred' has cataracts, he can't drive and his health isn't great. But he now has a flat of his own on the coast – somewhere to display his pictures of giant salmon and tell fisherman's tales to his new friends.

'Lucy'

When 'Lucy' left the Army to study for a degree she was optimistic about her future. The A-levels she had gained in the Royal Artillery had enabled her to get into university and she was on track to qualify in her chosen profession.

Confident after three years' service as a Gunner and a series of responsible telecommunications and security posts, the last door she expected to be knocking on after leaving the Regiment was that of a charity dedicated to helping the homeless. Not that 'Lucy' was ever on the streets, but she came perilously close to being.

So how did it happen? How did a bright, hard-working ex-soldier with a professional qualification and a good job end up desperate and broke? The stereotype of the homeless veteran is a middle-aged man with an alcohol dependency, or a young one suffering from PTSD.

The reality is that anyone can end up homeless or temporarily unable to cope, regardless of age, race – or gender.

The perceived stigma attached to homelessness makes many of the most unlikely people – senior officers or successful career women like 'Lucy' – reluctant to seek help. In her case, mounting debts built up because of high start-up costs and the fact that many of those she helped professionally were slow to settle their bills. Unable to pay her rent, and with no recourse to family help, she faced eviction.

Looking back, 'Lucy' says: 'I was suffering from clinical depression at the time and my tenancy in my old place was coming to an end. A friend offered to let me stay at his house for a while, but unbeknown to me his wife wasn't too happy. Six weeks later I went back to a locked door – at 11 in the evening.

'I went to all the public and charity organisations as I was literally homeless. The council said I wasn't a priority as I wasn't vulnerable enough. Shelter gave me the number of other shelters. I contacted the Royal British Legion but they couldn't see me for a number of weeks. I was sofa surfing for about ten days. The next place I was to go to fell through so I called the RBL again they referred me to Veterans Aid.'

She came perilously close to joining the ranks of the capital's rough sleepers. Within hours of arriving at VA, 'Lucy' had been reassured, guaranteed aid and had two sources of charitable funding identified. Her worst fears were never realised; her professional colleagues never became aware of her desperation.

Lucy is not typical of those who find themselves sharing tea and tears with the team at Victoria; luckily she was directed to people able to step in before her problems got worse. 'I was very relieved. The prospect of sleeping on the streets of London was very scary. I was upset, and ashamed that I had got myself into that position, but so very grateful to everyone who helped me sort out my accommodation problems.'

⇨ Information from Veterans Aid. Visit www.veterans-aid.net for more.

© Veterans Aid

VETERANS AID

Ex-servicemen in prison

'Myth-busting' inquiry delivers final report on former Armed Service personnel in prison

The Howard League for Penal Reform's *Inquiry into Former Armed Service Personnel in Prison* has today (Thursday 23 June) published its final report in the run up to Armed Forces Day on Saturday 25 June.

With official estimates suggesting that English and Welsh prisons hold around 3,000 ex-servicemen, there is public concern as to why those who have served their country go on to offend.

Theories have been put forward that the numbers of ex-servicemen in prison are on the increase, that ex-servicemen may be more likely to end up in prison than the civilian population, that recent action in Iraq and Afghanistan is significantly contributing to the rise of ex-servicemen in prison and that, in particular, it is combat-related trauma which is driving the crime that ex-servicemen commit.

> **With official estimates suggesting that English and Welsh prisons hold around 3,000 ex-servicemen, there is public concern as to why those who have served their country go on to offend**

The inquiry has found little or no evidence to justify any of these theories. The numbers of ex-servicemen in prison appear broadly similar to previous estimates, although there is no definitive survey available, and statistics suggest that ex-servicemen are less likely to be in prison than civilians. Ex-servicemen in prison are disproportionately older compared to the general prison population, and have offended many years after discharge. While post-traumatic stress disorder (PTSD) is a condition which does afflict a significant number of service leavers, there is no evidence that PTSD can be directly linked to offending behaviour.

Chair of the inquiry Sir John Nutting QC said: 'To a degree this inquiry has been involved in a process of "myth-busting". Ex-servicemen are not committing crimes shortly after leaving the plane from Helmand, and it is unlikely that combat trauma is driving criminal behaviour. The reality is that most ex-servicemen resettle into the community without problems but that for some, issues arise later in life which can lead to offending.

'The issues that lead ex-servicemen to offend appear to be much the same as most adult male prisoners, with social exclusion, alcohol misuse and financial problems afflicting both groups.

'While the numbers of ex-servicemen in prison appear stable, evidence from statistical surveys in both England and Wales and the United States show that ex-servicemen are more likely to be serving sentences for violent and sexual offences than the general prison population.

'Given the serious nature of these offences, it is therefore welcome that there is a huge amount of support available in the community for ex-servicemen. As well as resettlement provision on discharge provided by the Government, there are over 2,000 service charities dedicated to helping ex-servicemen in crisis.

'The problem our inquiry has encountered is that ex-servicemen in prison are often not aware of the help available. As they have offended many years after discharge, they have effectively "dropped off the radar" of those that can assist them. It is therefore imperative that those working in the criminal justice system can identify ex-servicemen and help them access the specialist support that is out there.'

In order to address this problem, the inquiry has made a number of recommendations. These include the expansion of the current free Veterans Helpline provided by the Service Personnel and Veterans Agency (SPVA). The main focus of this helpline is to provide advice on matters such as pensions and it operates during the working day from Monday to Friday. The inquiry recommends a significant expansion of this service into a crisis helpline, open 24 hours a day, 365 days a year, which would include ex-servicemen who can advise fellow veterans in crisis and point them in the direction of the many organisations which exist to help them.

The inquiry also recommends an expansion of existing efforts among the police, probation and prison services to identify ex-servicemen at the earliest possible point and put them in touch with ex-service organisations that can help them. In particular, the successful Veterans in Custody scheme should be extended to every prison in England and Wales.

25 June 2011

⇨ The above information is reprinted with kind permission from the Howard League for Penal Reform. Please visit their website at www.howardleague.org for more.

© *Howard League for Penal Reform*

From hero to zero

Michael Clohessy returned from Iraq with a distinguished war record – and ended up in prison. Our jails are swollen with former soldiers. Why can't they stay out of trouble?

By Ed Caesar

When the sniper opened fire, Michael Clohessy reacted first and fastest. It was the summer of 2004, and the 26-year-old private from Walton in Liverpool was serving with the 1st Battalion the 22nd (Cheshire) Regiment in Basra. In the clipped assessment of one officer, he was 'a cracking soldier, super-fit, bags of potential, and very mature'.

Indeed, during the Battalion's deployment at Basra's Old State Building, when the British Army were engaged regularly by insurgents, Clohessy had more than proved his worth.

So, when a sniper started taking pot shots at a joint British Army and Iraqi police patrol on a patch of wasteland, Clohessy knew what to do. He shouldered an injured Iraqi policeman and took him to safety behind a nearby wall, before pushing two of his colleagues, who had momentarily frozen as bullets thudded around them, out of harm's way. He then moved into the open ground and returned fire on the enemy with his machine gun. 'I don't know whether I hit him or not, but I pretty much took down the building with him in it,' he remembers. Either way, the sniper was silenced.

Nine months later, Clohessy stood before a judge at Liverpool Crown Court, on trial for grievous bodily harm with intent and affray. He had just begun his second tour of Iraq when he was pulled home to appear in the dock. The court heard that Clohessy had committed a violent assault outside the Barlow Arms pub in Walton, in Liverpool, on 31 December 2003, at a New Year's Eve party that had gone haywire. His victim, William Littlemore, suffered a fractured skull and permanently impaired vision as a result of the attack.

During the proceedings, the court also heard about Clohessy's valour. He was, said his barrister, a hero who had 'saved the lives of two young soldiers and also an Iraqi policeman' in a display of great courage. Nevertheless, the soldier was found guilty and sentenced to six years in prison. The judge took one year off his term on account of his service. He spent three years 'rotting in a b*****d cell' before being released in 2008.

Clohessy has since returned to the streets of Walton where he grew up. When we meet, he is unemployed, psychiatrically unstable and bitter. Physically, he does not betray symptoms of breakdown – he is fit and tanned, with close-cropped hair, large ears and a flashy smile. But he drinks heavily. During our interview, he downs vodka with a friend before noon. His mother, who now sees him rarely, thinks he is also using cocaine.

When Clohessy speaks, he does so in rapid-fire bursts, before losing concentration. The tour of Basra with the Cheshire Regiment was, he says, the only time in his life when he felt a true sense of purpose. But when he closes his eyes he can still picture dead Iraqis. He can still smell the cordite from expended rounds. He remembers being particularly shaken when he was assigned to collect the body of Gordon Gentle, a 19-year-old Royal Highland Fusilier, whose Snatch Land Rover was hit by a roadside bomb in Basra. An official inquest would later say that Gentle's death was avoidable – the Army had failed to install an electronic countermeasure against IEDs called element B onto his vehicle, which might have saved his life – and his mother, Rose Gentle, is now one of Britain's most vocal anti-war activists. Clohessy remembers kicking her son's boot as he lay in the hospital, and battling with the reality of what he was witnessing. 'Jock was alive this morning,' he says. 'Now he's dead. I thought, "What the f*** is going on here?"'

Clohessy tells me he is prone to fits of guilt and depression that started in prison, when he was locked up with nothing to do but 'go over and over in my head about the war', and which continue to this day. Four years ago, after a series of violent incidents and flashbacks, he was diagnosed with post-traumatic stress disorder (PTSD) by a doctor who visited him in prison. Sometimes his rage becomes so intense that he shuts himself in his house and refuses to see anyone for days. Meanwhile, he struggles to maintain relationships, including his relationship with the mother of his six-year-old son. This is unsurprising: Clohessy sleeps with a sword under his pillow.

We send too many ex-servicemen to prison. How many, nobody is sure. A recent study by the National Association of Probation Officers (Napo) estimated that there may be as many as 8,500 ex-servicemen in prison out of a total prison population of 92,000. Harry Fletcher, assistant general secretary of the organisation, believes that around 8% of Britons in jail are from the forces. The vast majority of these offenders are from the Army, and a large majority of the ex-Army are from the infantry. But other groups have taken issue with Napo's findings. The Ministry of Justice and the Ministry of Defence conducted their own survey, which they published in January, concluding that only 3% of the prison population were former members of the military – around 2,500 veterans in total.

Who to believe? Fletcher brought attention to the issue after hearing anecdotal evidence about the problem. He conducted his own inquiries via email with probation officers. On the basis of his calculations (supported by the fact that America's ex-service prison population is around 9%), Fletcher believes the Government has underplayed the numbers.

Certainly, the issue was striking enough for the Howard League for Penal Reform to begin an inquiry. 'We began on the basis of the Napo figure, which has now been cast into doubt,' says Andrew Neilson, of the Howard League. 'But I suspect the truth is that the figure is somewhere between 3% and 8%. And that still makes servicemen by far the largest occupational group in prison. That is well worth investigating.'

What the Howard League have found, so far, is arresting. There is a widespread belief that PTSD, occasioned by Britain's engagement in two brutal wars, is behind the large numbers of veterans who offend. The truth is muddier. PTSD normally takes several years after the traumatic event to set in.

Simon Wesseley, a professor of psychological medicine and principal investigator at the King's Centre for Military Health Research, found that in 2006, only 2% of Armed Service personnel suffered from PTSD (Combat Stress thinks the figure is 4–6%). Alcohol abuse was the main problem among soldiers, followed by depression.

Tim Riley, of the Braveheart Programme – a charity that analyses post-service stress as well as helping ex-servicemen to adjust to civilian life – believes that the 'statistics surrounding PTSD are very misleading'. But he will admit that many different types of stress are lumped together when talking about soldiers leaving the Army, including such mundane things as buying one's first house, and that 'we need to get some real facts right and look at the thing holistically'.

'The truth is, and always has been with the Armed Forces, that we recruit from poverty,' says Dr Hugh Milroy, CEO of Veterans Aid. 'It is a fact that many of these guys return to poverty when they leave. Guys join often with horrific backgrounds. The Armed Forces do amazing things, because they take someone from that background and they make something of them. But the problems often start when they go back to their old context.'

Consider Michael Clohessy's context. Walton is one of the most deprived areas in the most deprived city in England. Walk the terraced streets where the soldier grew up, the oldest of five brothers, and you get a sense of the deep poverty that afflicts the neighbourhood. Metal casing covers the windows of abandoned houses. Crime, particularly violent crime, is rife. This is a bastion of the white working and non-working class. The percentage of employment-age adults on benefits in the constituency was, at the last count, 28.9% – the highest in the country.

When Clohessy was a kid, he loved sport – 'I was always interested in training, and in football, and all that' – but found it difficult to concentrate in class. He thought he might be able to do a physical job, and the Army appealed. His grandfather and two of his uncles had been in the services, and they encouraged him to join up. 'They said it might be the life for me,' remembers Clohessy. 'And it was.'

Clohessy joined the King's Regiment at 16, and immediately excelled. He was 'Best PT' – best at physical training – in both phase 1 and phase 2 of his 36-week training course. When he joined the Battalion, aged 17, he was made a PTI, a physical training instructor, despite being 'only a baby'. He loved his job, and over the first years of his Army career he felt, for the first time, that he was doing something at which he excelled. But, when Clohessy was 20, he left the Army to go home and help his mother.

'She was having a bad time with my dad, it had got very domestic, a bit violent,' says Clohessy. 'She needed help with the babies [his four younger brothers]. Plus, I'd met a girl, and I thought maybe I didn't want to be in the Army, I wanted to be with her.'

During his four-year spell away from military life, Clohessy worked as an instructor at a local gym. He liked his job, but hated the world he had come back to. 'Once I'd come out, I realised I'd made an absolute bad mistake,' he says.

'I couldn't handle it on civvy street.'

The family also experienced tragedy in this period. In 1999, Michael's father, Lance, was working as a stonemason when there was an accident. Five tonnes of marble slipped from his wagon and crushed a co-worker named Joe Glover to death. Joe had already lost his brother, Ian, at the Hillsborough tragedy ten years previously, and the accident happened at 10am on Joe's first day at work since the disaster. The guilt associated with the incident would not leave Lance alone. 'He went round the bend,' remembers Michael. 'He lost the plot and hit the ale. That was it with him. He ended up moving away. Things got bad between him and me mum.'

So, Clohessy knew about guilt and trauma and bereavement long before he went to war. Dr Ian Palmer, a professor of military psychiatry, argues that it is a soldier's past that needs analysing when considering any case of post-traumatic stress. A difficult childhood or early exposure to trauma makes them more vulnerable. 'Recruits,' he says, 'bring all their life experiences, strengths, personality traits and coping mechanisms into service with them.'

Clohessy was not, naturally, thinking along these lines when he rejoined the Army in 2002 as a 24-year-old private in the Cheshire Regiment. He signed up because 'I wanted my old life back, and I got my old life back. It was the best decision ever.'

However, in 2003, having completed most of his pre-Iraq training on Salisbury Plain, he returned home on leave for Christmas. On New Year's Eve he went to the pub with his brother, Joseph. They became engaged in an argument, and then a fight, in which, says Michael, 'I protected my brother.

'He was my own flesh and blood. What was I going to do – let him get his head stamped on? I lost control. I destroyed the guy. At the end of the day, I reacted to a threat in a way that the Army had taught me to react. I was looking out for my own… That's the way the Army trains you.'

It took more than a year for Clohessy to stand trial. He left for Iraq with the case and the threat of imprisonment hanging over him. It did not, as his colleagues have testified, inhibit his performance. A villain in Walton became a hero in Basra.

We want our heroes spotless. Unfortunately, they don't come like that. They come like Michael Clohessy, a lad from a bad part of town. Clohessy says that, before we spoke, he had never fully discussed – not even with his family – the pain he is now going through. He has tried to explain it to doctors, but they 'look at me as if I've got three heads'. I ask him to describe the pain to me.

'I can't sleep,' he says. 'I feel guilty for the shootings that I done out there. I argue with myself all the time. Flashbacks started in prison, but now they get worse and worse. I'll go over contacts [engagements with the enemy] in my head, left, right and centre. I can remember every contact that I ever had, clear as anything. I can remember my feelings when I first shot someone dead.

'I feel embarrassed. I try to tell me own mum, and she doesn't know what to do. I'm a grown man. I was meant to be a lean, mean killing machine, as they say, and I'm crying out for help. Deep down I'm the shadow of the man I used to be. I'm breaking inside.'

Where Clohessy's story gets complicated is this: the war in Iraq had nothing to do with the incident that sent him to prison. He did not commit an offence because he had suffered from trauma – at least, not because of the trauma of war. The trouble with analysing why people offend is that no life story ever submits to easy diagnosis. Would Clohessy have spent time in prison if he had never joined the Army? Has his service made him more predisposed to committing in the future? We are lost in a sea of hypotheticals.

In any event, Clohessy is now a man with few options. It would clearly be a bad idea to put him in an office environment. Meanwhile, the skills that were useful in the Army are no use to him now. Machine-gunners are not in demand on civvy street, not even in Walton. When I ask him how he earns money, he says he lives on benefits. Others in the area tell me he is 'up to no good'. Certainly, Clohessy has not been able to keep his nose clean. He says he remains 'very aggressive'.

We send too many ex-servicemen to prison. The reasons why we do so are manifold and complex, and to address them will require attention to detail. Certainly, the problem of ex-servicemen in prison goes well past the remit of the MoD.

'The Army only takes people who come through the gate,' says Tim Riley, from the Braveheart Programme. 'Those people are a reflection of society as a whole, and what the Army does is to train people – to change men.

'It has to. We need people to think independently, to be different. One of the great psychological problems that these guys have [when they leave] is that they look at their old mates with disdain. Because they have different values now, and it further compounds their anger and frustration.'

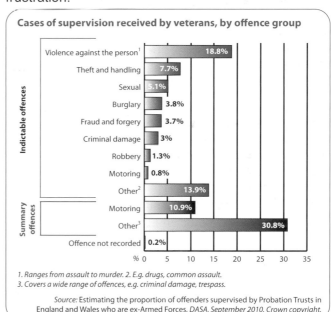

Cases of supervision received by veterans, by offence group

Indictable offences
- Violence against the person[1] — 18.8%
- Theft and handling — 7.7%
- Sexual — 5.1%
- Burglary — 3.8%
- Fraud and forgery — 3.7%
- Criminal damage — 3%
- Robbery — 1.3%
- Motoring — 0.8%
- Other[2] — 13.9%

Summary offences
- Motoring — 10.9%
- Other[3] — 30.8%
- Offence not recorded — 0.2%

% 0 5 10 15 20 25 30 35

1. Ranges from assault to murder. 2. E.g. drugs, common assault.
3. Covers a wide range of offences, e.g. criminal damage, trespass.

Source: Estimating the proportion of offenders supervised by Probation Trusts in England and Wales who are ex-Armed Forces, DASA, September 2010. Crown copyright.

What we need to ask is this: do we still want these tainted soldiers, warts and all? Do veterans deserve more than the average citizen, even if their past is chequered? They may have made bad decisions in their life, but they also made the decision to fight in a dusty, vicious conflict, waged on a specious premise, for paltry money, without question.

Michael Clohessy says he served his country, and that has to be worth something. He fought the war, and now the war fights him.

This piece is an extract from an article which first appeared in The Times *newspaper, 4 April 2010*

THE TIMES

⇨ If you're under 18 when you join the Army, you can leave by giving 14 days' notice at any time after you've been in the Army for 28 days – provided this is within six months from the day you join. (page 1)

⇨ All soldiers get a minimum of 38 days' holiday each year. The Army calls this 'leave'. (page 2)

⇨ In the immediate aftermath of a traumatic event, it is normal for people to experience some of the typical symptoms of PTSD. However, if symptoms are prolonged for more than one month, a clinical diagnosis of PTSD might be made. (page 4)

⇨ Psychologists have discovered that just over one in five servicemen on deployment showed signs of psychological distress and less than four per cent showed signs of post-traumatic stress disorder (PTSD). (page 5)

⇨ A comparison study between UK and US Armed Forces proved that US personnel suffered higher rates of psychological ill health, presumably because US personnel are deployed for longer and more frequently. (page 6)

⇨ In 2010, a total of 187 deaths occurred among the UK regular Armed Forces, of which 30 were serving in the Naval Service, 136 in the Army and 21 in the RAF. (page 9)

⇨ The MoD has completed a review into the policy that excludes female members of the Armed Forces from carrying out ground close-combat roles and decided that it should remain unchanged. (page 12)

⇨ The UK is one of a handful of states – fewer than 20 – which still recruit 16-year-olds into their Armed Forces. (page 15)

⇨ The Strategic Defence and Security Review will lead to reductions in manpower over the next five years across all three services and the civilians in defence. The Royal Navy will reduce by around 5,000 personnel, the Army by 7,000, the RAF by 5,000 and civilians by 25,000. (page 17)

⇨ The Military Covenant was conceived as an expression of the mutual obligations which exist between the nation, the Army and each individual soldier. It made clear that those who serve should expect to be treated fairly, to be valued and to be respected, in recognition of the extraordinary commitment and sacrifices which they were called upon to make. (page 25)

⇨ Under the terms of the Armed Forces Covenant, veterans will be entitled to a card which, while it will not act as a form of identification, will give them access to commercial discounts and privileges. (page 27)

⇨ Territorial soldiers and officers train in their spare time to provide support to full-time regular units when they're needed. From doctors and nurses in field hospitals to infantry soldiers working on the front line, most Army jobs are open to Territorials. (page 30)

⇨ Every year, 24,000 people leave the Armed Forces. (page 31)

⇨ Former members of the Armed Forces will become mentors to young people in schools across England following a £1.5 million grant to the charity SkillForce, Education Secretary Michael Gove has announced. (page 32)

⇨ The incidence of mental health issues arising from military service is a major issue; since 2005, for example, the charity Combat Stress has reported an increase of 72 per cent in the number of former military personnel seeking help. Their current workload includes over 4,400 veterans. (page 33)

⇨ The Ministry of Defence (MoD) has revealed that it is to offer post traumatic stress disorder therapy to help service personnel. (page 34)

⇨ Official estimates suggest that English and Welsh prisons hold around 3,000 ex-servicemen. (page 36)

Armed Forces Covenant

Also called the Military Covenant, this refers to the mutual obligation which exists between the United Kingdom and its Armed Forces. In practice, this obligation means ensuring servicepeople and veterans are not disadvantaged by their service, and where appropriate, are granted the right to special treatment. The Covenant existed for many years as an informal understanding between the Armed Forces and the state, but as of 2011 a written formal document has been in place.

AWOL

This stands for 'absent without leave'. It refers to a serviceperson who has absented themselves from their military duties without the appropriate permission to do so.

Barracks

A large building or group of buildings used to house soldiers.

Civilian

Anyone who is not a member of the military.

'Civvy street'

An informal phrase sometimes used by servicepeople and veterans to describe life and work outside of the military ('civvy' being short for 'civilian').

Close combat

In a battle situation, this refers to fighting between two combatants at short range.

Deployment

The movement of military personnel into an area of operation (such as a combat zone).

Discharge

A discharge is given to a member of the Armed Forces when their obligation to serve is over, releasing them from duty. There are different types of discharge, including Honourable and Dishonourable.

Leave

A serviceperson's paid holiday allowance – 38 days' holiday per year is the minimum for soldiers – is referred to as 'leave'.

Operations

Military actions in response to a developing situation or crisis.

Post traumatic stress disorder (PTSD)

PTSD is a psychological reaction to a highly traumatic event. It has been known by different names at different times in history: during the First World War, for example, soldiers suffering from PTSD were said to have 'shell shock'.

Regulars

Soldiers and officers of the regular Army ('regulars') are full-time military personnel. The regulars are distinct from those who serve in the Territorial Army, who train in their spare time.

Strategic Defence and Security Review

The SDSR was published by the Coalition Government in October 2010. It has caused much controversy, outlining large-scale budget cuts and redundancies within the Armed Forces. However, the Government says these are necessary for the Ministry of Defence to eliminate its estimated £38 billion deficit.

Territorial Army

Territorial soldiers and officers train in their spare time to provide support to full-time regular units when they're needed. There are two types of Territorial Unit – Regional and National. Regional Units train on week nights and some weekends and recruit from the local area. National Units tend to be more specialised and recruit people with relevant experience from all over the country. Because members travel further to get to training, they don't train on week nights. Most Army jobs are open to Territorials.

Veteran

A former serving member of the Armed Forces, in particular one who has given service during conflict or in time of war (more widely, the term 'veteran' is sometimes applied to anyone who has had long service in a particular field – people often talk about 'a veteran actor', for example).

accommodation, soldiers 1
aircraft carriers, budget cuts 21
Armed Forces, merging 22–3
Armed Forces Covenant 24–7, 28
Army, impact of Strategic Defence and Security Review 18
Army life 1–2

CBT (cognitive behavioural therapy) for PTSD 34
charities, care for wounded troops 7
cognitive behavioural therapy (CBT) for PTSD 34
contact with families, service personnel 2
cuts to defence budget, 17–19, 20–21, 22–3, 28

deaths, in Armed Forces 9
DeBique, Tilern 13–14
defence budget cuts 17–19, 20–21, 22–3, 28

EMDR (Eye Movement Desensitisation and Reprocessing) 34
employment of ex-service personnel 32
Expand SkillForce Core Programme 32
ex-service personnel 31–9
    finding employment 32
    homelessness 35
    mental health 33–4
    as mentors to young people 32
    in prison 4, 36, 37–9
Eye Movement Desensitisation and Reprocessing (EMDR) 34

food in the Army 1

holiday (leave) 2
homelessness, ex-service personnel 35

injured soldiers, care for 2, 7, 8–9, 10–11

leave 2
leaving the Armed Forces 1–2, 31–2
    under-18s right of discharge 16

medical care for wounded personnel 2, 8–9, 10–11
    post traumatic stress disorder 3–4
mental health problems 3–4, 5, 6
    ex-service personnel 33–4
mentoring of young people by ex-service personnel 32
merging the Armed Forces 22–3
Military to Mentors programme 32
mortality rate 9

motherhood and the Army 13–14

NHS treatment of PTSD 3–4
Nimrod cancellation 21

pensions, soldiers 2
post traumatic stress disorder (PTSD) 3–4, 5
    therapies 34
prison and ex-service personnel 4, 36, 37–9

recruitment age 15–16
rehabilitation 8–9, 10–11
resettlement packages 2
restructuring of Armed Services 17–19, 22–3
role of armed services 20–21, 29
Royal Air Force and Strategic Defence and Security Review 19
Royal Navy and Strategic Defence and Security Review 17–18

schools, ex-service personnel as mentors 32
sex discrimination 13–14
staying in touch with families 2
Strategic Defence and Security Review 17–19
    criticism of 20–21
support for Armed Forces personnel 24–7, 28–9
    Armed Forces Covenant 24–7
support for ex-service personnel 31–2
    homeless 35
    injured 7
    mental health supports 33–4
    with post traumatic stress disorder 3–4

Territorial Army 30

under-18s in the Armed Forces 16

veterans see ex-service personnel

women in the Armed Forces 12–14
wounded soldiers, care for 2, 7, 8–9, 10–11

young people
    mentoring by ex-service personnel 32
    recruitment into the Armed Forces 15–16

Zero Exclusion Pilot programme 32

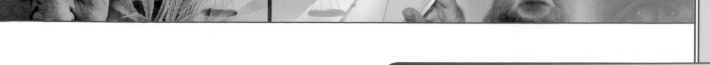

The publisher is grateful for permission to reproduce the following material.

While every care has been taken to trace and acknowledge copyright, the publisher tenders its apology for any accidental infringement or where copyright has proved untraceable. The publisher would be pleased to come to a suitable arrangement in any such case with the rightful owner.

Chapter One: Military Matters

Frequently asked questions about the British Army, © Crown copyright is reproduced with the permission of Her Majesty's Stationery Office, *Service-related mental ill health,* © Combat Stress, *The UK Armed Forces – past, present and future,* © King's College London, *Servicemen in Iraq less stressed than emergency services in Britain,* © Telegraph Media Group Limited 2011, *UK charities struggle to cope with wounded soldiers,* © Independent Catholic News, *'Surgery saved my hand after bomb blast',* © Crown copyright is reproduced with the permission of Her Majesty's Stationery Office – nhs.uk, *Deaths in the UK regular Armed Forces,* © Crown copyright is reproduced with the permission of Her Majesty's Stationery Office, *'I lost my leg in Iraq',* © Crown copyright is reproduced with the permission of Her Majesty's Stationery Office – nhs. uk, *MoD completes review into women in close combat,* © Crown copyright is reproduced with the permission of Her Majesty's Stationery Office, *Bearing babies and bearing arms is always incompatible,* © Guardian News and Media Limited 2011, *Catch 16–22,* © Coalition to Stop the Use of Child Soldiers, *Under-18s' right of discharge,* © Coalition to Stop the Use of Child Soldiers, *Strategic Defence and Security Review published,* © Crown copyright is reproduced with the permission of Her Majesty's Stationery Office, *The Strategic Defence and Security Review: a criticism,* © ConservativeHome, *It's time for Britain to merge its Army, Navy and Air Force,* © Telegraph Media Group Limited 2011, *Armed Forces Covenant 'an historic breakthrough',* © Royal British Legion, *The Armed Forces Covenant,* © Crown copyright is reproduced with the permission of Her Majesty's Stationery Office, *Some observations on the Armed Forces Covenant,* © DefenceManagament. com, *Yes, we owe our Armed Forces – but Cameron's leaky law is not enough,* © Guardian News and Media Limited 2011, *What is the Territorial Army (TA)?,* © Crown copyright is reproduced with the permission of Her Majesty's Stationery Office.

Chapter Two: Life After Service

Leaving the Armed Forces, © TheSite.org, *Ex-military to be inspiring role models for young people,* © Crown copyright is reproduced with the permission of Her Majesty's Stationery Office, *Veterans' mental health,* © Mental Health Foundation, *MoD offers PTSD therapy,* © British Psychological Society: www.bps.org.uk, *Veterans and homelessness,* © Veterans Aid, *Ex-servicemen in prison,* © Howard League for Penal Reform, *From hero to zero,* © Times Newspapers Ltd.

Illustrations

Pages 2, 13, 27, 30: Don Hatcher; pages 5, 11, 22, 31: Simon Kneebone; pages 7, 21, 29, 33: Angelo Madrid; pages 12, 19: Bev Aisbett.

Cover photography

Left: © Nic Kilby. Centre: © Rotorhead. Right: © Martin Kessel.

Additional acknowledgements

With thanks to the Independence team: Mary Chapman, Sandra Dennis and Jan Sunderland.

Lisa Firth
Cambridge
September, 2011

ASSIGNMENTS

The following tasks aim to help you think through the issues surrounding the Armed Forces and provide a better understanding of the topic.

1 Find out about the unrest in Luton in 2009, in which a parade organised as a mark of respect to soldiers killed in action was interrupted by a group of Islamist protestors objecting to the Afghanistan war and the alleged actions of British soldiers. Debate the various issues raised by this incident in small groups. Should the protestors have been prevented from demonstrating on the grounds of distress caused to the families of the soldiers and the public? Or should their rights to free speech and peaceful demonstration be protected? Do you think homecoming parades for soldiers are a good or a bad idea?

2 Find out about the condition of PTSD throughout history, beginning in the First World War. How was 'shell shock' diagnosed and treated? How has the way this illness is perceived changed since the early years of the 20th century? Do you think there is still a degree of stigma attached to this problem? Write a summary of your research findings.

3 Read some of the poetry written by soldiers during the First World War. Some war poems, such as 'The Soldier' by Rupert Brook, speak of the pride the authors felt for the cause they fought for. Others, like 'Dulce et Decorum Est' by Wilfred Owen, describe the horrors of war. Compare the language used in two contrasting war poems, attempting to put yourself in the soldier's situation and empathise with his feelings. You could also try writing your own poem about service during the First World War.

4 Read 'Mrs Dalloway' by Virginia Woolf, focusing in particular on the character of Septimus, the war veteran struggling to cope with PTSD, and the way in which his condition is treated by the medical establishment of the day. Write a review of the book and its portrayal of PTSD.

5 'This house believes it is not appropriate for young people under the age of 18, who are not able to join the police or watch an 18-rated war film, to nevertheless be allowed to join the Armed Forces.' Debate this motion in two groups, with one group arguing in favour and the other against.

6 Read 'Gulf', a novel for young people by Robert Westall. Write a review, focusing on what you feel the book has to say about soldiers on either side of a war who are caught up in the bloody conflict.

7 Read *Ex-servicemen in prison* on page 36 and *From hero to zero* on pages 37-39. Why do you think some ex-servicemen go on to offend? Discuss your views in pairs.

8 Read *Veterans and homelessness* on page 35. Choose either 'Fred' or 'Lucy' and write a fictionalised first-person account of their life after leaving the military: how they ended up homeless and how their lives eventually got back on track with help from the charity Veterans Aid.

9 Find out about the operations in Iraq and Afghanistan. What gave rise to the conflicts in these regions, and what part do British service personnel have to play? How many UK troops are currently stationed in these areas? Write a summary of British involvement in each conflict.

10 Watch the film 'The Hurt Locker' and write a review, focusing on how the characters portrayed are affected by their experiences in a war zone.

11 Read the articles on pages 12 to 14. What is your opinion on the role of women in the Armed Forces, and in close combat roles (from which they are currently excluded) in particular? Do you think this amounts to discrimination, or is it a sensible policy in a battle situation? Write an article summarising the current situation and giving your views.

12 Read the articles on pages 24 to 29. What is the Armed Forces Covenant? Do you think it is right for members and former members of the Armed Forces to be given special treatment in certain situations? Write an essay discussing your views.

13 What is the Strategic Defence and Security Review, and why has it been controversial?

14 Find out about the work of the Territorial Army and write a summary of how they operate and in what way they complement the regular Army.

15 Using articles from Chapter Two and the website www. civvystreet.org.uk, create an illustrated booklet aimed at those about to leave the Armed Forces, entitled 'Life on Civvy Street'. Make sure you include information on where former servicepeople can look for help and support.

16 Watch the final episode of the BBC TV series 'Blackadder Goes Forth'. How does this manage to combine humour and poignancy in its portrayal of war?